LEADERSHIP RESET

LEADERSHIP RESET

HOW SELF-AWARE LEADERS DRIVE CULTURE AND GROWTH

MEHER MIRCHANDANI

LAUNCHPAD

An imprint of
Srishti Publishers & Distributors

Srishti Publishers & Distributors
A unit of AJR Publishing LLP
212A, Peacock Lane
Shahpur Jat, New Delhi – 110 049

editorial@srishtipublishers.com

First Published by Launchpad,
an imprint of Srishti Publishers & Distributors in 2025

10 9 8 7 6 5 4 3 2 1

Printed and bound in India.

To my entire team at Palmon Group and my family.

Thank you for trusting me, for walking beside me, and for embracing a culture-driven, conscious path to success.

Your courage, faith, and unity—despite all odds—made this journey meaningful.

This book is for you.

If you want to go fast, go alone.
If you want to go far, go together.
— *African Proverb*

CONTENTS

INTRODUCTION

Love Your Business and It Will Love You Back

An organization or business is a way of life; it is where we spend the major part of our waking hours. It is where we learn, grow, and share. It is what gives meaning to our lives, so how can it not be led consciously and with love? With this intent, I go to work every day, and I am intrinsically motivated by the sheer joy of being part of the working force of the world. I want to be the best version of myself so that I can contribute to my team members, my family and all my stakeholders.

This book is my journey and mission to make the workplace a haven where everyone who is part of it is thriving, not just surviving.

My journey towards self-love and awareness is directly correlated to the unparalleled growth and transformation that I was enjoying in my family business. I attribute this success to a radical mindset shift that had occurred within me. I was becoming aware of the role that self-love played in a person's life in all areas. And after this realization, I put a lot of effort into changing my company's culture and add love as a key element of every action we took and every decision we made.

The dynamics of any business begin to shift when we start to lead with self-love. Even the most obstinate of challenges are overcome, the risks come off as less scary, and you have the confidence to persist for longer despite the odds. The impact of self-love is far greater than what we are led to believe. The first area that it impacts is at a personal level. And at its very core, the deep connection to oneself makes a person feel alive and soaring.

> *The relationship that we have with ourselves determines the quality of all our relationships.*

And that reflects on the kind of accord we have with our spouse, children, friends, and lastly, the people at work. When I stepped into my family business, it was a time that greatly challenged me to go within myself and develop a deep level of self-love and awareness, which eventually helped me shine within the organization despite the numerous odds that were stacked against me.

The fact that I led with self-love helped transform the business and the rigid culture that had been that way for years. I saw the business change, transform, and evolve right before me as I fell in love with myself. Today, our company's culture is all about love. Everybody honours love within the organization. And there is a palpable shift in energy.

This is the only way real leaders can impact, influence, and inspire their teams. It's natural that when you constantly work on growing yourself as a leader, your team will follow suit. I firmly believe that the top leadership in an organization creates a great or a not-so-great culture.

Self-love enables you as a leader to lead with authenticity and allows you to connect with your team at a much deeper level. Authentic expressions take on a different meaning altogether. And in the process, you learn, as I have, that vulnerability is a strength, not a weakness. Additionally, leading with self-love offers an exceptional quality that only a very few leaders possess. It allows you to be genuinely and wholeheartedly invested in your team's growth at a very individual and human level. It's only natural for high-level performance to follow.

Performance is a by-product of growth. When I took the helm of the family business, I initiated the restructuring process by engaging external coaches and establishing a coaching programme within HR to provide consistent guidance and support for our team members' growth. At a different level, this kind of leadership can have a significant impact on the organization overall.

1

AWARENESS

Challenges and Obstacles

You can overcome anything. You can completely recreate yourself. Nothing is permanent. You are not stuck. You've got choices. You can think new thoughts. You can learn new things. You can create new habits. All that matters is that today you choose never to look back.

—Brad Turnbull

People are surprised when I tell them that a deep, unshakeable and permanent sense of unhappiness has lived with me for almost all my adult years. It was a feeling I could never quite understand. And it remained with me even though my parents loved me deeply and I had access to the very best of everything.

I frequently travelled around the world, wore expensive clothes, dined at the finest Michelin-star hotels, studied at the best private institutions and was chauffeured in Mercedes S-Class and Rolls-Royce everywhere.

And still, it would be years before I would discover that a lack of self-love is at the root of all my misery. At a professional level, I had precisely zero impact. I felt like a square peg in a round hole when I joined my family business in 2013. It was a tumultuous time in my life, both personally and professionally.

My family's business had quickly grown from a single operation in Jafza to a successful group of more than 20 companies. At one point, our manufacturing facilities were producing a million pieces a month for clothing stores such as the Gap, BHS, CNA, Debenhams and several others across the US and Europe. The operations that had started with just one factory had quickly grown to 30 factories that employed over 4,000 workers with sales offices in New York, London and Manchester.

The Challenge

When I joined my family business, it was to add value and contribute to the group. By then, the company had grown radically and was dealing in kitchen appliances, office furniture, facilities management, real estate and investments. I was appointed as the managing director of the group and charged with the responsibility of growing the business further.

As soon as I joined the fast-expanding business, I realized that it was nothing like I had imagined. The company was bureaucratic, traditional, and lacked effective reporting and processes. It was also male-dominated. There were no HR policies or dedicated HR managers who could instil a solid company culture. While my father, the chairman and CEO of the group, loved his people, contributed to their livelihood and understood their pain, it seemed to me that the lack of transparency and processes led to him being taken advantage of in several instances.

The middle management, who had been with the company from its early years, was comfortable with the status quo and either ignored or challenged the changes I wanted to introduce within the company as I took the helm. This made me feel very vulnerable. I thought that I could not make any positive difference within the company despite my best efforts.

From hiring the right talent to training and aligning them to running the divisions, everything became more challenging. For example, when I took charge, I hired a manager for our facilities management company, and the team refused to report to him. After a few months, I was forced to let him go.

The finance director, who had been part of the company since its inception, felt threatened when I took the helm. She refused to make amends and upgrades to the ongoing financial processes. She didn't share any reports with me, which made it difficult for me to understand the financial position of the company.

As I spent more time within the organization, I realized that the company that my father had so lovingly created now lacked vision, mission and strategy. Its culture was not clearly defined or maintained, which, I felt, made it impossible for me to add value to the business. I thought I wouldn't even last a year within the organization. I was having a hard time understanding what made us financially successful because, except for the founder, there was nothing unique about the business.

Despite having founded and grown my fashion label over the last 12 years, and having a proven track record of solid performance, growth and employee satisfaction levels, I was not able to fit into the Palmon Group. My brother had worked in the business for 10 years and then parted ways with it to start his own F&B venture because of these very challenges.

He had also felt like an outsider looking in. No doubt, it was a difficult moment of choice for him. The company had somehow ingrained the status quo, and the culture was very difficult to change. But change, as I've come to understand, is the only constant in life. And the Palmon Group desperately needed to change. Within the first few weeks of coming on board, I realized that the group was not ready for the next generation of leaders.

My father had more readily accepted the fact that my brother had walked out of his business, but it had been 5 years since then.

I kept thinking about what would happen if I also had to part ways with the Palmon Group. And if I decided to persist, would my father allow me to contribute to the business? Will he be willing to trust in me and let go of the traditional way of working that wasn't serving the company anymore?

Even if my father agreed to the cultural shifts I wanted to introduce, I didn't know where to start. There are so many elements that come together to help a company function optimally—growing and motivating your people, getting the reporting structure right, getting the right people to take on key responsibilities, creating and improving the company culture and more.

I say this with a lot of love, respect and endearment for my father, who was and still is a very gifted, intelligent, courageous and passionate business person and leader. He is why we were able to grow to this level in the first place. But for the company to go to the next level and position itself as a global leader, everything needed to evolve for the better.

As I now look back and reflect on what went on, I can say that the primary reason the company had grown despite the aforementioned problems was that my father was very action-oriented and personally invested in every aspect of the business. The company hinged on his leadership and presence for survival, with no systems or processes in place. But I knew that exponential growth depended on the team.

The Learnings

The book *What Got You Here Won't Get You There* by Marshall Goldsmith highlights these points beautifully. Goldsmith recognizes that sometimes leaders can unknowingly hold on to unhelpful behaviours and traits that can impede growth. His book offers insightful lessons about characteristics that grow a company, but at one point actually start getting in the way of leaders and keep them from having even more success. This book greatly helped me understand how to move forward.

When I took charge of the company, there was no concept of weekly or monthly meetings. The only thing that happened once a year was an audit. I had no idea where the company was headed.

As a leader, it is crucial to understand how the company is performing month on month to get a holistic view of what's working and what needs to change, the steps that need to be taken to reduce costs and steer the company in the right direction. A leader can't even begin to add value until they know where things stand.

Mind you, dear reader, that it wasn't only the challenges I was facing in the business. I was also facing personal challenges. How could I help the business or stand in my power if I didn't know I had any? I didn't know myself and hadn't cultivated my leadership abilities by then.

The realization that the company and I both needed help was the first step towards my awareness. Let me simultaneously share my path, as they are both connected. When I learnt that success is something you attract by becoming the person you want to be, as taught by Jim Rohn, that's when I started making shifts in my personal life, which eventually led to creating major shifts within the business.

> *In every adversity lies the seed of an equal or greater opportunity.*
>
> —Napoleon Hill

My journey to radically transform the quality of my life was a long series of small steps and decisions. A few years before joining the family business, I had started learning Theta healing. It's a form of meditation that brings your brain into a deeply rested state called 'Theta' and enables the practitioner to bring massive mental, physical and emotional shifts within.

I became a healer and, after a few years, started teaching this form of meditation to others. The process gave me so much joy and mental peace that I decided to invest more time in exploring other options.

Next, I learnt Basic DNA, Advanced DNA, DNA three, Manifestation, Intuitive Anatomy, and Basic, Advanced, and Intuitive Instructors, dug deeper and invested time in several other programmes. Through these programmes, I learnt that we can reprogramme the subconscious mind and eliminate self-limiting beliefs to recreate a new reality and a new outcome in our lives. It taught me to meditate and shift beliefs at the Theta brainwave. I began to recognize the thinking patterns and belief systems that were significantly hindering my happiness and progress. Slowly, I started to develop a sense of self-love and self-awareness that had been missing from my life till then. I started noticing patterns of thought that weren't serving me.

In late 2013, the same year I joined my family business, I applied to the Entrepreneurs Organization (EO). The ethos of this member-led global organization put me on the path to becoming a conscious leader. EO's holistic framework supports entrepreneurs and enables them to excel in business, family, community and personal life. The organization provided me with great insights and lessons into life and business. With the help of learning events and my EO forum, I was able to start evolving myself, my life and my leadership abilities.

I was meeting peers and business leaders from different walks of life. Their perspectives and experiences were starting to add immense value to my life, and I was getting better equipped to navigate the business with more knowledge. Through conversations with fellow members and lots of introspection, the realization that I do not love and accept myself emerged. I discovered that at the deepest level, my lack of self-love had been the core of my misery all these years. And these beliefs were now causing me to fail in leading my family business as well. This awareness pushed me to start making the change in myself to become a victor instead of a victim.

Becoming a Leader for Good

I developed a laser-sharp focus on growing as a leader. I attended dozens of events offered by EO, the Harvard Business School, London Business School, Singularity University, and those led by world-renowned speakers, entrepreneurs, and gurus such as Ron Kaufman, Ryan Avery, Jay Shetty, Jim Collins, Vishen Lakhiani, and several others.

One of the key learnings that stood out was a masterclass that I took from Ron Kaufman on the value of uplifting service. It changed the way we were serving our clients and impacted our bottom line in a very positive way. Ryan Avery's 'Words to delete' talk on communication and about the power of speech was also a game-changer that showed me how to be a better and more effective leader and how to be a strong communicator for the teams and people who looked up to me. I started to negotiate better with my stakeholders, customers and teams. These tools helped put me on the right path to transform the company culture.

My learning over the years helped me become a 'leader for good' instead of just a good leader. I started understanding my strengths and also got a much better view of my weaknesses. I also started gaining perspective on how family businesses are run with the help of the Insead Leadership School's *The Family Enterprise Challenge* by Randel Carlock.

This programme enables families to learn and grow together, providing life-altering insights into other family-run businesses through case studies. It allowed me to create my values and chart out a parallel planning process map for the company and family. The more I learnt about leading a family business, the more I could share and contribute to the growth, strategy, vision, mission, values and people of our company.

During this time, I was also actively contributing to the entrepreneurial community. I was speaking regularly on various platforms and also learning to excel in business. I was taking on leadership positions, like being on the board of EO. As I applied those learnings within my family business, I started to see remarkable shifts in the business that unfolded right before my eyes.

The results I was seeing encouraged me to help other people the same way I had helped myself. In the intent to formalize my contribution in 2019, I embarked on the journey of coaching. I became a transformative Certified Professional Co-Active Coach from the Coaches Training Institute (CTI), which is one of the largest and most established professional coach training organizations in the world.

The programme helped me connect with my consciousness and gave me the tools to effectively communicate and serve the world. I also pursued neuro-linguistic programming and became an NLP practitioner. NLP helps change thoughts and behaviours to achieve desired outcomes.

As an entrepreneur, your team is the first group of people you motivate to live better, and I did that with 100 per cent dedication. So, by growing into a better version of myself and learning from different leaders, I started gaining authentic power on all fronts of my life.

I was able to bring my whole self to the business; there were no layers. I was able to be an authentic leader, and I could lead with love. For me, leadership and life are one—you have to be the same person at home and work. There's no disparity between the two roles because that's when you can serve your company, its people, and yourself.

The Awakening

As written and proven, a one-degree change is all that is needed to move a mammoth ship towards a different destination. That is exactly what I did. By 2017, it had already been 5 years since I had joined the Palmon Group. I was working on building the culture, growing the business and also actively exiting businesses that were not our core.

Once I set direction with the North Star (vision), the values and mission, everything became clearer. I was able to lead with my heart. I felt liberated and fell in love with the process of doing business. I recruited new members who could thrive within the new culture. I got on board a process and culture manager who would help me hold the culture across the organization. With her knowledge on yoga, consciousness and people management, together we were able to make a bigger shift in mindset. I started Mindfulness Monday meeting with my entire team to start the week with positivity and enthusiasm by speaking about topics concerning personal growth.

This was the time when my name started appearing regularly on the Forbes list of next-generation entrepreneurs in the UAE, among other coveted spots. When we know better, we do better. Knowledge can be so very powerful, and I learnt it first-hand. It not only gives you confidence but also empowers you to lead with conviction.

Slowly but surely, my father started accepting new ways and adapted to the new realities of business and leadership. But most importantly, he recognized that what had brought us here could not take us any farther. He had started softening up to the new processes, reporting and structure that I was putting in place.

During this phase in my life, I learnt many valuable lessons about entitlement and how leaders who feel entitled find it hard to achieve long-term success in business. The mental attitudes of entitlement lead to selfish and self-serving beliefs and behaviours, and make it hard to develop real relationships at work. This ensured I kept my feelings in check as I navigated the challenges of the family business. The same can also be said about ego and money. I learnt to detach myself from negative feelings and embrace the strength that lies in togetherness. Bringing people closer together and bridging the gaps, I realized, was my true role as a leader. This took even greater meaning because I was running a family business.

By 2018, I had recruited a new team member for every key role within the organization. My brother, Kunal Lahori, joined us again in the family business, and together we started a fund called the Manrre Logistics Fund. We embarked on a new journey to grow our assets and funds to a 275-million-dollar entity. We started at 75 million dollars in AUM, and we are now (2025) at 200 million dollars in AUM.

My purpose is to contribute to the well-being of my family and stakeholders and to impact each one of my team members positively. To do so, I constantly work to evolve myself into a better person and leader.

My journey taught me that the purpose of awakenings is to be aware of certain truths, love, and your true existence as a soul. To enable such an awakening, we need to be patient in the face of challenging situations. If the situation in our life is favourable to what we want, there will be no awakening. We go through emotional turmoil and feel the deepest pain, fear, rejection, abandonment, guilt, doubt and a lot more because we have to work on these issues so true awakening can take place. As soon as the new me took birth, my life evolved to a higher level. The path of challenge becomes grace, and this happens when we become aware that every circumstance and event in life is for our highest good.

When you are driven by love instead of ego, you are able to maintain and strengthen relationships with customers and suppliers. Let me share an interesting experience that highlights the benefits one can reap after bringing these changes to an organization.

My family business also deals in commercial, industrial and logistics properties. One of our tenants was constantly refusing to pay us. The rent had gone unpaid for three months by then. As a protocol, my team asked the tenant to vacate the premises, but he refused.

We saw no resolution to this problem. When I learnt about the issue, I requested a meeting with this customer. During that meeting, rather than asking him why he wasn't releasing the payment, I took the opportunity to ask him what his pain was and how we could help him do his business with ease without interruptions. I apologize to him for sending a legal notice and a penalty notice. I also told him that we value him as a customer and that our only request is that he pay on time so we do not get penalized. I also told him that we would love for him to renew his contract instead of leaving on a sour note.

He was so bewildered by my attitude that he released the long-overdue rental payment that very same day and also renewed the contract for three more years. My father and brother were astonished to learn about this development and couldn't understand how I got to a person who, until just a few days ago, was not even willing to talk to us. Not just that, but he also happily released the payment that very day!

When you work from a place of love, without ego or judgement, great things can happen, and it becomes so much easier to overcome obstacles. This is the number one reason I'm able to close major deals and solve problems at their root level within the business. I don't wait for things to escalate. This is a strategy that always works in my favour.

I've also learnt that when businesses value their customer relationships over transactions, they always win. In our business, I value the customer more than the transaction. Now I want to share how other leaders can leave a positive impact on their families, communities and businesses as they lead from a place of love.

This book is dedicated to leaders who want to bring drastic changes to their businesses and their lives. It testifies to the fact that when you lead with self-love, it can transform your journey at a personal level as well as a professional level. Bring self-love to the centre of all your endeavours and undertakings, and feel the palpable shift in energy. That is what changes the game for you and your team.

ACTION STEPS

Instructions: Take a quiet moment to reflect on your journey

1. Awareness Check-In

"The first step toward change is awareness."

- What are three recurring challenges I am currently facing in my personal or professional life?

1. ____________________
2. ____________________
3. ____________________

- What emotions are tied to these challenges (e.g., frustration, fear, confusion, sadness)?

____

- What patterns or beliefs may be holding me back from overcoming them?

____

2. Leadership Self-Reflection

"Success is something you attract by the person you become."

—Jim Rohn

- What kind of leader do I believe I am today?

____

- What kind of leader do I aspire to become?

____

- In what areas do I need to evolve to bridge this gap?

____

____

____

3. Turning Pain into Power

"In every adversity lies the seed of an equal or greater opportunity."

—Napoleon Hill

- Recall one moment when you felt powerless. What did you learn from it?

___

- How can I start leading with more love and less ego in my current situation?

___

Commitment to Self

Write one intention or promise you're making to yourself today, inspired by what you've read:

I commit to: ______________________________

____

Pause. Breathe. Acknowledge the shift.

Let this reflection be your starting point to lead with awareness, courage, and love.

2

ACCEPTANCE

The Relationship Between Love and Leadership

One can live magnificently in this world if one knows how to work and how to love.

—Leo Tolstoy

A few years ago, at the Palmon Group, we reached a point where the business was growing, but something felt off. We were expanding our operations, taking on larger projects, and hitting our financial targets—yet there was a certain disconnection I couldn't ignore. People were getting the work done, but I didn't see the spark. The energy in the office felt transactional.

That's when I decided to shift my focus inward—not just toward the numbers, but toward the people behind them.

I began holding regular one-to-one meetings with each head of department. These weren't just operational check-ins—they were deep conversations about leadership, emotional intelligence, and the kind of culture we wanted to build at Palmon. I shared my vision of a workplace rooted in trust, compassion, and self-respect. I talked to them about the power of love in leadership—how connection, empathy, and mutual care are not "soft skills" but critical foundations for sustained success.

Some were sceptical at first—we'd all been conditioned to believe that emotions don't belong in business. But over time, these leaders began to understand that what I was asking for wasn't sentimentality—it was *humanity*. They saw how fostering a more connected team could unlock performance in a way rigid KPIs never could.

To bring this energy into everyday work life, we made space for more human moments. We began celebrating every team member's birthday—not just with cake and gifts, but with team reflections and small appreciations. People started to open up, smile more, and share their stories. These small gestures, over time, built a more profound sense of belonging.

We also introduced regular team-building games. Sometimes they were structured, sometimes completely spontaneous. Whether it was problem-solving challenges, silly office games, or even cooking competitions, the goal was the same—to let people drop their guard, laugh, and reconnect with one another beyond their job titles.

The shift was gradual but undeniable. Teams started collaborating more freely, communication became more open, and people felt seen. The culture began evolving organically, from a place of duty to a space of shared purpose.

One moment that stayed with me was when a long-time employee came to me after one of our birthday gatherings and said, "For the first time, it feels like we're not just employees—we're part of something bigger." That's when I knew we were on the right path.

This experience reminded me that love in leadership isn't about grand gestures—it's about consistent, intentional efforts to connect. It's in the one-on-one conversations, the celebrations, the shared laughter, and the trust you build through daily interactions. At Palmon Group, that shift toward a culture rooted in love changed everything, not just for the business, but for the people who bring it to life every day.

I've known leaders who dislike the words 'love' or 'self-love' and don't believe they have any place in a business setting. But in my experience, I've found this to be very untrue. Love, including self-love, has cornerstone significance for the business world. And I've seen firsthand that remarkable things can happen when we blend love and business together.

I will showcase how self-love and leadership must go together if you intend to grow your business and transform its culture for the better. I will also share how love transforms the experience your stakeholders have with your company and share examples of the many global organizations that utilized this philosophy in their day-to-day business functions and turned their fates around.

Love has cornerstone significance across various fields, but very rarely is love, including self-love, deemed important in matters of business. I find this quite strange, considering that we dedicate a major portion of our lives to our professions.

In fact, over the decades, love, or any semblance of emotion in business, was always considered to be a sign of weakness. Business leaders are finally recognizing the importance of 'love' in business and how this emotion can literally transform the very 'soul' of their companies.

Regardless of your field of expertise or how 'technical' it may be, it is good to remember that we are always in the people's business. Human beings are primarily emotional creatures, and when guided and inspired, they are assets that can potentially transform a business.

And it's not just my belief. Organizational research confirms this as well. Most notably, a study by Sigal Barsade and Olivia O'Neil shows that a culture of love within an organization can directly correspond to increased feelings of job satisfaction and teamwork. And we all know that happy employees create happy customers. But unlike what you may envisage, leading with love in the work context is not all rainbows and butterflies. Self-love and leading a business with this mindset are just as much about being comfortable with conflict and difficult conversations.

Martin Luther King described it so aptly when he said, "Power without love is reckless and abusive, and love without power is sentimental and anaemic." In a strictly business context, an expression of love is seen at various levels of the business.

People ask me all the time how they can bring love to their organizations. My simple answer is that love is already there. Start by tuning into it. Its presence can be felt during a regular day at work and measured in small interactions throughout the day. An appreciation for an employee's contribution to a project, assistance for a struggling co-worker, a smile, a simple act of gratitude, and more. It's about compassion and empathy.

Culture eats strategy for breakfast.

—Peter Drucker

This powerful quote says it all. It highlights the significance of setting the right culture in a company. Regardless of how great your strategy or how remarkable the company goals may be, without an ingrained culture of love, your business will struggle to bring great results regularly.

Culture works as a nurturing ecosystem or habitat for your business strategy. The right culture supports people within the organization to meet their goals. In my experience, a culture of love within a company always leads to sustained success. Culture also determines how your employees act in critical situations, how they cope with pressure, navigate the various challenges at work, and eventually, how they treat their partners, colleagues, and customers.

A company's culture is usually created by the top management, and it is often done unknowingly. When it comes to cultivating culture, their actions speak louder than words. The relationships that the upper management builds with employees have a trickle-down effect throughout the company.

This is not to say that company culture is definite. It is complex and ever-changing. But it often depends on the moods and feelings of the people who define it. It is not uncommon for higher management to focus on the financial and rational side of the business, often at the expense of other important areas. Failing to incorporate the right culture, in this case, a culture of love, means the business strategies may not work as well. This naturally leads to subpar results and stunted growth.

The Importance of Being in Love with Your Business, Stakeholders, and Employees

Love has a strong influence on workplace outcomes. Whether it's your employees or stakeholders, the more love they feel, the more engaged they become. Unfortunately, very few managers and business leaders focus on building that kind of culture.

The impact of compassionate love has been observed in various industries, from financial services to real estate, with the same results. If your intention is to take your organization to the next level financially and otherwise, and all you expect from your employees is teamwork and innovation without building the necessary emotional culture to support that growth, your organization will grow slowly, if at all, after a certain point.

It is not uncommon to see that many top leaders across organizations believe that love can potentially undermine important business variables and key performance indicators, including productivity levels, quality of output, competitiveness, efficiency, and others.

Therefore, it is easy to see why organizations focus primarily on these qualities instead of working to include love in their businesses. On the flip side, I can confidently say, based on what I've experienced in my family business, that the aforementioned indicators naturally improve when love becomes part of your organization's fabric. To top it all off, a loving attitude can help develop continuous goodwill and deeper relationships at the workplace—a sure-fire way to enjoy rapid business success.

> *Customers will never love a company until employees love it first.*
>
> —Simon Sinek

It is also important to note that when you are connected with yourself, you naturally connect well with others. As a conscious leader at the helm of your organization, you can instil this culture throughout your business. But the change starts with you. We aren't just leaders when we run businesses; we are leaders in multiple areas of our lives.

You don't have to be a business leader to apply and reap the rewards of these principles. If you are a mother, you are a leader. You can be a leader in your health and fitness, and in your growth. We are all leaders in our lives. And as a leader, you are always inspiring someone else; in my experience, leading by example is the most powerful.

As a leader in a second-generation family business, if I come in at 10 am to work every single day and expect my team to be in the office before 9 am, it can be considered hypocritical. So, I make sure I come in at 7:30/8 am to inspire my team to be on time, ready, and charged.

By staying connected with myself, I'm able to lead with my heart. We have created the company values manifesto, and I always ensure that the company's top leadership is aligned with those values. We always refer back to these values in meetings, emails, etc. I always encourage my entire team to ensure that they are following the company values that are rooted in love, respect, and appreciation, and it always helps.

At this point, I'd like to illustrate how a lack of solid company culture, one that is driven by emotions other than love, can take companies down. Lehman Brothers offers a great example. Founded in 1850, the firm was famous for its high-level culture and focus on service and value creation first and profits second.

As a family enterprise, the company's internal culture was also founded on a premise of trust, mutual respect, and love. The bank was known for not just lending money to its clients but also taking serious care of their stakeholders and building partnerships that helped their clients grow.

But in 1969, after the demise of Bobbie Lehman, the last member of the original founding family, the company's culture began to shift. New performance metrics were introduced, and profit and growth became the sole focus and purpose of the company's existence. As a result of several bad decisions and a declining internal culture, the bank struck disaster and ceased to exist after 2008.

In toxic environments, workers struggle to perform well. Research also confirms that managers are closely connected to a work culture, and most employees quit their jobs primarily because of the managers. A communication breakdown between managers and workers is one of the most basic signs of a toxic workplace. Moreover, high employee turnover has huge costs for a business.

Take the example of IBM. Its bosses believed the company was untouchable thanks to its people and an innovative culture. They saw their workers as special free spirits who challenged the doctrine and were ready to think out of the box in a quest for new and better products. That was all good and well, except that this culture did not exist in reality.

There was, in reality, stifling bureaucracy at the mid-level of the company that had squashed the independent spirits under regulation and red tape. Conformity was expected, and those who failed to do so were forced out. During this time, IBM leaders also did not realize that smaller, more agile competitors were grabbing their market share. By the 1990s, IBM was on the verge of bankruptcy. At this point, Lou Gerstner was brought in as the new chairman. It took him 5 years and thousands of layoffs to turn IBM around.

Building a Great Company Culture Is Impossible—Without Emotion

A company culture where compassion, collaboration, creativity, transparency, and teamwork take precedence is bound to succeed. None of it is possible in a cold, mechanical, and rigid corporate environment. Employees are a company's true hallmark, and the company culture is put to the test when things go wrong.

Take the example of the Red Cross. In 2011, an employee sent a tweet on the organization's official account by mistake, which was meant for her account. The offending tweet stayed on their official account for at least an hour before it was taken down.

The original tweet read as, "Ryan found two more 4-bottle packs of Dogfish Head's Midas Touch Beer. When we drink, we do it right #gettingslizzerd."

The employee who made the mistake was not fired. Instead,

the tweet was removed, and in its place, a humorous message was shared by the Red Cross, which read, "We have deleted the rogue tweet, but rest assured, the Red Cross is sober and we have confiscated the keys." The humanitarian organization also followed it with a blog post.

The tweet was widely shared and also led to the Dogfish Beer Company encouraging people to support the Red Cross. This started a sort of impromptu collaboration between the Red Cross and the Beer Company that encouraged many donations in the following weeks. Red Cross's adherence to its values of compassion and creativity turned the incident into a great fundraising opportunity that garnered widespread appeal.

Another top-rated company, Xerox, was saved from bankruptcy because of its spectacular culture. When Anne Mulcahy became CEO in 2000, the company was $18 billion dollars in debt. On top of that, a 26-point stock nosedive made advisers push for a declaration of bankruptcy. Someone also suggested that the Xerox culture (which involved lots of freebies for employees) needed to be killed for the company to survive.

Mulcahy ended up meeting with the company's top 100 executives personally. She informed them about the dire straits that the company had fallen into. 98 of those 100 employees committed to helping rebuild Xerox, and most of them are still with the company today. Within the next 8 years, the company had paid off its debt, revamped its product offering, and upgraded to a better, more sustainable business model.

Mulcahy truly believed that the loyalty of customers and employees could turn a company around, and that is what helped change the fate of Xerox. It all goes back to the fact that happy, committed, and loyal employees are the lifeblood of a solid business.

Here's another remarkable story that illustrates the Ritz-

Carlton's great company culture. The luxury hotel chain owes a big part of its fame and glory to its gold standard of customer service. They offer outstanding lessons in service, teamwork, and a never-give-up attitude that the company has successfully ingrained in its employees.

A family that was staying at the Ritz-Carlton Bali was carrying special eggs and milk for their son, who had severe food allergies. When they reached the hotel, the eggs had broken and the milk was spoiled. The Ritz-Carlton staff went out of their way to make the family comfortable.

The manager and the staff looked for the specific eggs and milk throughout the local town, but they weren't available. The hotel's chef knew that they could find both items in Singapore, which was half a world away. The chef contacted his mother-in-law and requested her to fly to Bali and bring the eggs and milk with her.

Imagine the level of cohesion and teamwork that existed among the employees for them to go out of their way to such an extent to make their customers happy. This is only possible with great culture. What are the building blocks of great culture? It starts with empowering your employees, trusting them, embedding your values, creating the proper emotional infrastructure, and finally, building resilience so the teams can cope with changes.

In all of the above stories and hundreds of other similar ones, leaders prove that the more connected they are with themselves, the better their relationship with everyone around them and the faster they can turn the fortunes of their companies around.

The Process of Inculcating Love in Your Company

Inculcating love in your company is one of the most important decisions you will make in your business. As illustrated above, a great culture can make an organization, and a lack thereof can just as easily break it. Its presence allows companies to scale new heights, and its absence can plummet organizations even when they are already at the top. Here is a simple process that will help you inculcate love in your company.

1. Adopt self-love and encourage it organization-wide

You have to start by inculcating a culture of self-love in your company. As a leader, you will need to adopt it first, so employees learn as much from your actions as they do from your teaching. Developing self-love can prove to be a vital skill for your entire life in general, but also more specifically, it can significantly aid you in your professional journey.

When you employ it as a business leader, you gain more clarity and remove the mental clutter or emotional baggage that impedes your happiness and progress. The same applies to workers putting their heart and soul into the company. Encouraging self-love is a simple step that will enable you to produce more leaders within your organization who are ready to take charge and become change makers for good.

For this, meditation, learning, gratitude, journaling, and repetition are the tools at your disposal as you begin to develop self-love and encourage your teams to do so as well.

2. Who you are is what your company will become

Another ingredient, as you find ways to inculcate love in your company, is to find your 'why' as a leader. Because when you understand what drives you, it's easier to create the fabric of a driven and resilient company that understands its why (or purpose). As you begin to find your why, moving away from what sucks energy out of your life and closer to the values that are in alignment with your best visions of life will guide you. But before you can do any of that, ascertaining 'who' you are, as a person, as a leader, is the first step.

Once you've understood who you are and why, you can then become ready to inject that purpose into your company. There are many benefits to having a purpose-driven organization. Such organizations are more successful, and your employees become less fragile and more resilient. Purpose-driven businesses can revolutionize their industries.

3. Alignment

When companies are in alignment, they become ready to unlock their full potential. An aligned company is successfully able to create an environment of trust, manage complexity, and respond rapidly to all situations. It's an organization that works as a unified whole and reaches for the same overarching goals by overcoming the differences (between teams, individuals) and working off the same page.

Innovation alone isn't enough. A culture of innovation is impossible to sustain without alignment. An aligned organization is one where partners and stakeholders understand the company's vision and mission and stand behind them wholeheartedly. Aligned organizations understand their strengths and weaknesses and become formidable players within their industries.

4. Thrive—don't just survive

Love is the essence of this life. And it's at the core of all human beings. When we adopt self-love, find out who we are and our purpose, and bring alignment throughout our organization, we create the foundation required to thrive in our business and life truly.

You can thrive in your business when your communication

follows your company's core values, when you are not afraid to be vulnerable, when you live by your values, bring love in all your dealings, work to maintain deep relationships at work, continuously invest in yourself, and keep doing the good work by detaching yourself from the results.

Conclusion

Many business leaders believe that love and self-love have no significance in a business setting. But the truth is, when you blend love and leadership, companies grow and their cultures change for the better. The energy of 'love'—even in a business setting—is palpable, and building a great company is nearly impossible without this emotion.

It's easy to see why business owners or higher management in financially successful businesses often attribute their success to the product or service. And even though that may be true, at the end of the day, it's not 'just' the service and product. It's also how those services and products are provided and whether those interactions with employees, customers, and stakeholders are being held from a place of love.

It is entirely possible to reach a certain level of success through a stellar product or service alone. Still, if you genuinely want your business to reach the next level, or grow 20x its current size, your company's internal culture is what you will need to work on to achieve that kind of success.

ACTION STEPS

1. Self-Connection Check

"You can only lead others as deeply as you've led yourself."

Reflection:

- What are three ways I currently show (or withhold) self-love in my daily life and leadership?
  1. ______________________________
  2. ______________________________
  3. ______________________________

Action:

- What is **one self-love practice** I will begin today to support my growth as a conscious leader?

---

2. Culture Scan

"Culture eats strategy for breakfast."

—Peter Drucker

Reflection:

- How would I honestly describe the culture of my team or organization in one sentence today?

Action:

- What **one small, love-driven action** can I introduce this month to bring more connection, trust, or appreciation into my workplace?

3. Purpose Alignment

"Who you are is what your company will become."

Reflection:

- What personal value or belief do I want to see more of in my organization?

Action:

- What is **one way I can model this value more intentionally** in my behaviour as a leader this week?

3

UNDERSTANDING

Relationship with Self

Your whole life is the manifestation of the thoughts that go on in your head.

—Lisa Nichols

There was a time in my life when everything seemed outwardly successful—I was running multiple businesses, raising my daughters, and managing my home and work like a well-oiled machine. But beneath the surface, I was disconnected. I was constantly doing, striving, pushing—without checking in on *how* I was doing. I wasn't aware of what I needed emotionally, mentally, or physically. I was simply in survival mode.

Then life started sending me signals—or rather, warnings.

It began with a sudden vertigo attack that landed me in the hospital for three days. I brushed it off as stress. Then I caught a persistent cough, but I didn't slow down. I kept pushing, showing up, performing. That cough led to torn cartilage in my ribs—an injury that took six months to heal. Still, I didn't pause. Not really. My body was screaming for rest, for attention, for acknowledgement, and I was still too busy to listen.

Then came the car accident.

It was in that moment, sitting on the side of the road with my hands shaking and my heart racing, that something inside me cracked open. I had been ignoring all the signs. I realized I wasn't just overwhelmed—I was in self-sabotage mode. I was betraying myself every day by not listening to my inner needs, by putting everyone and everything else first, and by staying disconnected from my truth.

The confusion that followed pushed me to explore deeper healing. I found myself drawn to past life regression therapy—something I'd never considered before. But in that session, I saw clearly what I had been missing all along: *self-love.* Not self-care, not self-indulgence, not self-discipline—*self-love.* The deep, nurturing, unconditional kind. The kind that says, "You are enough, exactly as you are." The kind that holds you through your failures, that listens without judgement, that creates safety within.

That insight changed everything.

When I began practising self-love, things started to shift. I made space to rest without guilt. I communicated more honestly in my relationships. I stopped chasing achievement to feel worthy and started aligning my work with my heart. My health improved. My clarity returned. My relationships deepened. My businesses found a new rhythm—one led by intuition and trust, not fear and pressure.

The turning point in my life wasn't external success or validation—it was the moment I chose to stop abandoning myself. Self-connection became my foundation, and self-love became the missing piece that finally made everything make sense.

If there is anything that I've learnt while navigating the challenges of life and business, it is that it all starts with *you.* Whether you are a key decision-maker in your organization or an employee interested in sparking positive change, this advice remains applicable wherever you are within your business (or career).

If you want to be remembered as a true leader within your business, live and leave a legacy, touch lives or grow your business massively, the truth is that you cannot even begin this process until you have self-love at the centre of all your undertakings. The teachings in this chapter will show you that deep inner work precedes outward business success and that it is necessary to overcome our limitations and break free.

This chapter will showcase the significance of developing self-love at the deepest level and offer you valuable tools and insights so you can thrive at work and in your personal life. You will learn to unfold who you are and recognize childhood programming that is stopping you from fulfilling your destiny, letting go of everything that doesn't serve you and falling in love with yourself. This programme will guide you in connecting with yourself and learning to love yourself. It will also teach you that self-love is a prerequisite for giving love and positively impacting your life, leadership, and the organization as a whole.

So, are you ready to serve your soul and become a true leader?

Self-Love and How to Develop the Most Important Business Skill There Is

I believe that self-love is a way of being. It's a process of going within oneself and emerging as a much more powerful being. Unlike what we grew up to believe, love has nothing to do with the rest of the world or the love of another. It has everything to do with you. When you are in love with yourself, the universe is in love with you. Doors open, and wonderful coincidences take place when you least expect them.

As a leader in business, self-love allows you to gain clarity on life as a whole. It helps remove unnecessary mental clutter and emotional baggage that impedes your progress. The resulting ease puts you in a much better position to understand the 'why'—or North Star and true purpose—of your company.

Firms that find their purpose and connect with it can make a profound impact on the world. This has a cascading effect throughout the organization. As you continue to move in the right direction, you will realize that you are in a state of 'flow'. You are deeply enthralled with your journey and can strike beautiful and deeper relationships with stakeholders, partners and employees consistently.

So many times in life, we allow our ego to get in our way. The 'I' present inside us comes in the way of striking lasting partnerships, making stellar deals or holding on to exceptional people who are assets to the company. Over the years, I realized and honed the skill of differentiating the constant chatter inside my head (especially the negative self-talk) from the person that I was. This is the one thing that keeps most people in the world from achieving greatness. They stand in the way of their love, peace, happiness and progress—without even realizing it.

As a society, we are all collectively focused on financial achievements, awards, accolades and material success to the point that we completely neglect the 'soul'. Our spiritual growth plays a very important role in the quality of our lives. I often wonder why schools don't teach soul studies like Math and English. If we were taught about our minds and souls from an early age, each one of us would become loving and powerful beings, vibrating at much higher frequencies. And we would also be innately happy and peaceful.

Tony Robbins, the world's top business strategist and life coach, frequently talks about the science of achievement and the art of fulfilment. He says that financial achievement and growth are a science that anybody can understand and apply in a very methodical way to reap the results. But the art of fulfilment is just that—an art. A person can be successful and still be very unhappy, or vice versa.

I agree 100 per cent. A few years after I joined my family

business, my efforts were recognized regularly. In 2017, I was listed on the Forbes Next Gen list and regularly won prestigious awards. However, I did not feel proud of any of it. In fact, I still felt empty and unhappy. That is when I realized there was something deeper within me that I needed to conquer first. I was able to overcome this feeling at last after many years when I finally met myself and fell in love with the person I found.

I discovered that the relationship we have with ourselves determines the quality of all other relationships we hold.

Unfold Who You Really Are

The choices that we make today affect our evolutionary process. It is important to choose consciously so you can evolve consciously. In the words of Gary Zukav, "The purpose of this life and all its experiences is not to make ourselves what we think we should be. It is to unfold who we already are."

All the sages and wise people throughout history have stressed the importance of knowing the self. Can you imagine spending your life with a stranger you don't know (and may not even like)? Knowing yourself at a deeper level and developing self-love can bring a powerful authenticity to your life. It will help you command respect and love on a whole different level. We build relationships with people by getting to know them and spending time with them. But what are we doing to know ourselves? Are we spending time with ourselves?

The truth is that finding and knowing yourself is a lifelong process. As an entrepreneur or business leader, it becomes even more important because a great responsibility for the growth of the business and guidance and support for your team rests on your shoulders. The five things that catapulted my journey of knowing and loving myself included silence and meditation, journaling and gratitude, affirmations, reading and learning, and exercise. I recommend these steps to every single person reading this.

Making a connection with the self is not a one-off deal. Like you continue to learn about your spouse or business partner at a deeper level to enjoy a robust relationship, the same rule applies to you as well. You need to continue to invest time in learning about yourself.

Our Most Recurrent Emotions Are a Result of Childhood Programming

Life is meant to challenge you and stimulate your growth. Every challenge that comes to us at the various stages of our lives enables us to step up. When you awaken to this truth, you start to live with purpose. Most people constantly live in some form of emotional pain—the pain of not being loved, appreciated, heard and something else. But if truth be told, most of the pain that we feel as humans is self-inflicted.

When you take a closer look, you will realize that this hurt is often the result of childhood programming that we received at a very young age. These beliefs are so deeply rooted in our subconscious minds that we don't even know if it is possible to reverse this programming. But to grow and prosper, it is important to eradicate beliefs that don't serve you anymore.

What is pain? It is a low-energy feeling or vibration. It includes emotions such as fear, anxiety, jealousy, hatred, resentment, guilt and more. Often, these feelings stem from a deep-rooted thought of not being good enough. We need to work towards recognizing the triggers of negative and disempowering emotions and then weed them out. Awareness is the first crucial step on this journey.

I felt disempowered most of my life. For some, this feeling of helplessness and unhappiness can be permanent, as it was for me. Despite receiving the deepest levels of love, protection and attention, I have felt lonely almost my entire life. It was only a few years ago that I acquired the knowledge and developed the ability to uproot my negative beliefs. The negative emotions I had been feeling were a result of the programming I had received in my earlier years. Here's a powerful process by Joan Cusack Handler that you can use to identify beliefs that aren't serving you anymore.

Monitor Your Thoughts

Notice the feelings that you're having on a regular basis. Discern the most common or frequent ones. Push yourself past answers such as fine and okay, and try to probe deeper. Note each answer and don't rush through the process.

Identify the Triggers

Think about what may be triggering this feeling. Do you feel that there are certain aspects of your life that you may have no control over? Some events, thoughts or even dreams? Look for patterns that may be forming as a result.

Don't Judge Yourself

Feelings don't follow reason. Don't judge yourself for what you may observe as a result of this process. The fact is that life's events generate feelings. Even though we decide which feelings to attend to and which ones to ignore, we cannot unfeel things. It's important to give your feelings room to breathe.

Talk About Your Feelings

Vulnerability is not a weakness; it is a strength. When we share our feelings with ourselves and our loved ones, they shrink in size. The more we stifle a feeling, the stronger it becomes.

Live in the Moment

Unfortunately, most of us either live in the future or the past. Our past makes us sad, and our future makes us feel uncertain and unsure. But the truth is that every day is a new day. And we have the power to evolve and grow. A simple but powerful exercise that helps with this is to sit in a quiet place and centre your thoughts. The moment they sway, bring them back to the moment. Do this for a few days and you will realize that you are living in the moment and enjoying your day-to-day experiences much more.

> *If we live in the energy of the past, we will never be able to change our future.*

Identifying our feelings is an important part of this journey. If you're unable to single out specific subconscious patterns that are causing hurt and pain in your life or stopping you from taking yourself to the next level, don't be afraid to seek help from coaches or healers. I do it to this day because my life is my responsibility.

Reprogramme Yourself for the Better

Loving yourself allows you to be in strong and loving relationships with others. How you view yourself is how you view others. As mentioned before, most of our beliefs are shaped when we are children. The things that happen in our lives as we are growing up and what others say to us become imprinted in our subconscious minds. Over the ensuing years, these ideas become strong beliefs that we hold about ourselves, other people and the world that we live in.

A belief is an 'absolute truth' for the person holding it. Beliefs determine how you perceive and interpret the world. Beliefs are not facts. They are based on our perceptions of other people's attitudes, opinions, and thoughts that are communicated to us sometimes loudly, but often silently.

As we grow up, we don't realize that many of these beliefs or 'worldviews' don't serve us anymore. In fact, they are harmful to our well-being, prosperity and happiness and don't allow us to live a fulfilled life.

There are many ways to release negative beliefs. For me, an introduction to Theta healing is what began the process of change. I learnt about the biology of beliefs and their impact on our lives. It helped me dissolve many beliefs that weren't serving me. Additionally, the teachings of Dr Joe Dispenza and Dr Bruce Lipton helped me reinvent the person that I am today. I call this new me my 'soul self'. Over the years, I've worked, learnt and thought hard to identify the six habits that will enable you to transform your life and uproot negative beliefs.

Meditation

Meditation allows people to move beyond their analytic minds and into their subconscious mind, which is where the real magic happens. Meditation allows us to dig deeper into our thoughts, beliefs and feelings, and slowly but surely release them. It is a way to get in touch with your higher self.

Reprogramming

Real positive change in our lives happens when we reprogramme the subconscious mind. Our subconscious mind is the boss. It runs our lives. The reason why we do not see a difference in our lives despite staying positive is because that positivity—which is within our conscious mind—is not aligned with the beliefs of the subconscious. This is why we need to reprogramme. The subconscious mind is best programmed in the Theta state, which is the state just before you fall asleep. Using programming audio and affirmations in this state can help change your programming.

Learning
When you know better, you do better. Learning has to be a permanent aspect of your life, and knowledge is to the mind what oxygen is to the body. When we learn, we are able to view life from a different perspective and are able to make better choices.

Gratitude
Gratitude is one of the most powerful emotions in the world and raises your frequency. Gratitude enables you to receive more of what you are grateful for. It puts you in the ultimate state of receivership. Whatever you want in life, when you show up with gratitude, you attract the outcomes you desire.

Repetition
You need to practice these elements every single day to see a serious impact and change in your life. Repetition is the key to your success. Repetition allows us to create habits and reprogramme the subconscious.

Journaling
Journaling will enable you to release stress and negativity. It is also a powerful tool when you want to seek or offer forgiveness and move on, especially if you feel emotionally stuck in the past because of deep hurt.

The fact is that unless you change your energy by changing your beliefs, you will have a hard time attracting positivity to your life. Rapid and massive transformation requires that you connect with yourself every single day.

Get Ready to Serve Your Soul
Live your values. Be authentic. The only person whose opinion

matters in your life is you. When I started letting go of things, it filled my life with immense joy and courage. Breaking the habits connected with your old self is a sure-fire way to help the new you emerge. We are habituated to thinking and feeling a certain way. But to align yourself with your soul and become powerful beyond measure, you need to let those feelings go. And it will surely feel very uncomfortable because this has been your pattern for years. But life starts beyond our comfort zone, and letting go will allow you to discover peace beyond what can be expressed in words.

The truth is that we are the victims of our thinking patterns. It is also very easy to pin the blame on society, our family, colleagues or just about anyone (or anything) else for things that aren't working out. But real change happens when we take control and assume responsibility for our lives, especially for the things that aren't working out. It is only then that we can work to change them.

Once this process of letting go begins, one realizes that there is just so much weight (that we carry around unnecessarily) to shed. After we release the unwanted beliefs, we need to let go of our old habits, our thought patterns, material things and finally people and conversations that don't serve us.

In this journey, letting go of everything that doesn't serve you is a very important step. And it is very easy for us to fall back into our old patterns. The only way to remain the new person is to strengthen the new beliefs, habits and thinking patterns.

Time is limited and precious. Don't waste it living a life where you just exist. Choose to live fully and wholeheartedly. Always remember that success is something you attract by the person you become. Your personal growth will also precede your professional achievements.

Love Yourself Fearlessly

As I mentioned before, love has nothing to do with someone else.

It has everything to do with you. The feeling you feel when you love yourself is indescribable. Dust away all that you wish for yourself and look at yourself from the perspective of the divine. Humans have the ability to instantly transform their relationships by seeing the things they love, appreciate and are grateful for in another person. And the same can be applied to you. The world is not responsible for how you feel about yourself. You are.

You are here to create magic, and it begins the moment you begin to love yourself fearlessly.

The following exercises will help you love yourself more generously:

1) Write down ten things you appreciate about yourself.
2) Write down ten things you really admire about yourself.
3) Note down ten things you are proud of.
4) Write a love letter to yourself.

When you embrace the teachings shared in this chapter, you will find these four exercises to be extremely fulfilling. But remember, the books you read and the habits you create make you. But for that to happen, you need to be consistent in applying the lessons learnt.

You were born from love, into love, and we go back to love. Let's choose to live in love because that's the energy of the universe.

The more love you bring to your being, the higher you will evolve. As your energy becomes love, you will attract all that you need to live a fulfilled and peaceful life.

Let me share a story that perfectly illustrates the power of love. This was six months after we started the Manrre Fund. We were at a point where we wanted to end the contract with our fund manager. And while the fund management company had done a fantastic job with conceiving, launching, registering and managing the fund, there were some other services that the current fund managers were unable to provide, including fundraising.

So, we asked them if we could take a different route and terminate our contract with them a few months earlier. After a lot of back and forth, they came back to us and said that if we wanted to terminate the contract, we would still need to pay the remaining six-month fee, which was a hefty $55000 in total. Additionally, we were looking at 180 days of non-performance when we could clearly see that they could not raise the required funds for us.

We tried all kinds of negotiation tactics with them, but nothing worked. So I tried for the final time. This time, I sent them an email from my heart, saying that we have had a great relationship with them (which was true). They were the reason our fund got started the right way (this was also true). And we did not want either party to have any bitter feelings because we never know when we may cross paths again.

I also wrote that we valued their relationship far more than the transaction itself. And for the betterment of the fund, the best course of action would be to terminate the contract. The fact that I had spoken to them with so much love, gratitude and respect, after three days of silence, they came back with a yes. We ended up paying just a $5000 penalty for early contract termination, and that's all. Whereas, my brother proposed to involve a lawyer so he could find a way to terminate this contract. My perception is that a lawyer involves extra costs and extra administration, but an authentic email from the heart requires 10 minutes of my time, along with maintaining the relationship.

Coming Alive

Please remember that most of who you think you are is a 'borrowed' idea given to you by those who knew nothing about themselves. The pain you have felt most of your life is an illusion. And you have the power to release it. A great future is only possible when you embrace the present moment.

Coming alive means you believe with all your heart that you have always been enough. This life is a gift, and treating it as such is our responsibility. Be authentic, be courageous and live your life to the fullest. Remember, what you seek is always seeking you.

As we walk on this journey, we adopt and accept beliefs that weren't ours to have in the first place. Your mission in this life is to chisel away all that is not you so the real you can emerge. Once you let go of the energies, materialistic objects, people and situations that no longer serve you, you help accelerate the process of coming alive.

Here is my 5-step process of self-love:

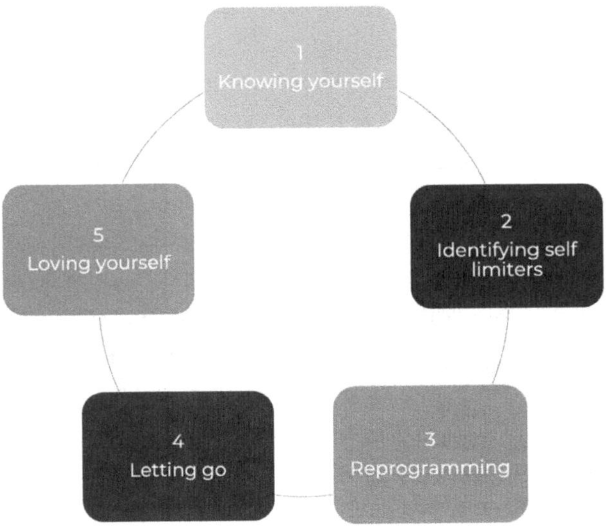

Ultimately, your purpose in life is to be in love with life, with yourself, and everything as it is in this moment. To feel grateful, to forgive and live in faith, not fear. We are spiritual beings having a physical experience in this world.

No matter where you are or where you start, put your judgements aside and learn to be aware and strive to become a better version of yourself. To evolve and become the person we are meant to be, we must elevate our words, actions and thoughts.

People often ask me how much self-love we should have. My answer to this question is that self-love can play a truly transformative role in your life, which is why you should have a lot of it! You should be focused on being committed to the process so that you can develop it at the deepest level. Self-love is the process of knowing yourself, connecting with your inner self, overcoming self-limiting beliefs, letting go of everything that doesn't serve you, and finally meeting and staying in love with the authentic you.

I'm also often asked if self-love can make you a narcissist or selfish. Narcissism and selfishness do not equate with self-love. They are, in fact, polar opposites. Some people love themselves so much that they only see their own self-centred benefit in everything they do. They want their ego boosted and want to take advantage of others around them.

With self-love, you understand that you're gifted and special in your own unique way. But you also respect others. Self-love is healthy, while narcissism is not. Self-love enables you to drop the ego and judgement and live authentically, and also contribute to the lives of the people around you. Self-love is when you prioritize yourself to grow and evolve.

This case study exemplifies how a strong organizational culture can be a powerful strategic asset, fuelling sustainable growth, attracting top talent, enabling successful acquisitions, and even inspiring new ventures. Lucy d'Abo's journey with DABO & CO is a testament to the transformative power of leading with values and clarity. I had the privilege of hosting Lucy on my podcast, and hearing her reflect on the immense fulfilment that comes from building something with heart was truly inspiring. Her story is not just about business success—it's about legacy, alignment, and the deep joy a founder experiences when culture becomes the soul of the company. It's a remarkable case that beautifully reinforces the core message of this chapter.

Conclusion

Loving yourself is not a milestone—it's a lifelong practice. As you continue this journey of self-awareness and healing, remember that every relationship you nurture, every decision you make, and every success you celebrate begins with how deeply you've connected to your own heart.

In this chapter, we learnt that developing self-love is an important part of your professional journey. As a business leader, it enables you to become more powerful, gain more clarity and remove the mental clutter or emotional baggage that impedes your happiness and progress. Meditation, learning, gratitude, journaling and repetition are the tools at your disposal when you begin to develop self-love.

ACTION STEPS

1. Where Have I Been Abandoning Myself?

Reflection Prompt:
Think of a recent time when you ignored your own needs—emotionally, mentally, or physically—to fulfil obligations or please others.

- What did you sacrifice in that moment?
- What signs (physical, emotional, intuitive) did you overlook?
- What would it have looked like to choose yourself instead?

Action:
Write a short paragraph on what you would do differently next time to honour your needs.

2. What Beliefs About Myself Are No Longer True?

Reflection Prompt:
Recall a belief you formed about yourself in childhood (e.g., *"I'm not good enough," "I must work hard to be loved,"* etc.).

- Where did it come from?
- How has it shown up in your personal or professional life?
- Is it serving the person you are today?

Action:
Write the old belief. Then, reframe it into a new empowering one (e.g., *"I am worthy just as I am."*).

3. How Can I Love Myself More This Week?

Reflection Prompt:
Self-love is a practice.

- What is one loving thing you can do for your body, your mind, and your spirit this week?
- What boundaries do you need to set to make space for this?

Action:
Create a "Self-Love Intention" for the week with one specific action in each area:

- **Body:** (e.g., Take a walk, rest early)
- **Mind:** (e.g., Journal, read a nourishing book)
- **Soul:** (e.g., meditate, practice gratitude)

4 PURPOSE

Knowing Yourself and Your Organization

> Your growth determines who you are. Who you are determines who you attract. Who you attract determines the success of your organization.
>
> —***John Maxwell***

We are all born with the desire to learn. But somewhere along the way—amidst the stress of survival, the pressure to succeed, and the fear of failure—we forget how important learning is to our growth, our joy, and our evolution. Learning is what allows us to move from where we are to where we want to be. Whether it's acquiring a new skill, gaining wisdom through experience, or deepening our self-awareness, growth happens when we choose to learn—consciously and continuously.

I truly grasped the transformative power of learning when I joined the Entrepreneurs' Organization (EO). At the time, I thought I was joining a networking group. What I discovered instead was a lifelong school for entrepreneurs, where peers became teachers and vulnerability was welcomed as a path to wisdom. I was exposed to business tools, leadership frameworks, and, most importantly, stories—stories of people who had failed, learnt, grown, and succeeded.

That experience awakened something in me. I realized that education is not just a privilege—it's a responsibility. I had access to resources that millions across the world did not. According to UNESCO, 244 million children and youth worldwide are still out of school. In low-income countries, only 20 per cent of children complete secondary school. In Sub-Saharan Africa, nearly nine out of ten children are unable to read a simple sentence by age 10. These numbers are more than statistics—they are silent cries for opportunity.

That's when I made a personal commitment: I would not only continue to educate myself, but I would make education the WHY of my company. Through every deal, every transaction, every success, a portion of our profits would go toward educating children who otherwise may never have the chance to learn.

We partnered with Jeev Sewa Sansthan, an incredible organization based in Bhopal that provides quality education to underprivileged children across India. When we began, we supported the education of just 20 children. Today, we have committed to serving 275 children, and currently sponsor 100 students on our journey to that goal. This is not just corporate social responsibility—it is personal. It is the purpose in action.

Learning changed my life. And I believe it can change the world.

As a leader, you must embrace the role of a lifelong learner—not just for yourself, but as a model for your team, your family, and your community. Read books. Join learning communities. Take courses. Attend seminars. Learn from mistakes. Learn from mentors. Learn from silence.

The moment you stop learning is the moment you start declining.

The most evolved leaders I know are the most humble learners. They know that wisdom has no finish line. When you commit to learning, you commit to growth. And when you commit to growth, the world opens up in ways you never imagined.

And here's something beautiful: when you learn, you evolve. And when you evolve, you begin to find clarity. That clarity brings you closer to your personal *why*. Once you uncover that, your company's *why* becomes clearer too. It is one of the most crucial things you can do to set your organization on the path to success—and to create a team that wholeheartedly stands behind the change they make in the world.

After embracing self-love in my life and championing it within my organization, the next natural step was to make education our company's *why*. It was through learning about perceptions, about myself, and about the world that I understood the importance of loving myself first. That shift is what allowed me to uncover my purpose.

When I meet leaders (and I meet many of them), only 1 in 20 can clearly articulate why they exist, what truly drives them, or why their company exists. Yes, they may be doing good deeds or contributing to society. But charity without clarity rarely brings lasting fulfilment. A clear *why* only emerges when you know your ultimate purpose in life.

My purpose emerged when I began to love myself. It led me to my *why*, and eventually helped me discover my company's *why*.

Today, I want to contribute to humanity through coaching, speaking, and writing. I want to create awareness about the importance of self-love, so that people can love, live, and give—with no expectations from others—and move toward deep fulfilment.

This is my why. This is what drives me.

Why Does Your Company Need to Be Purpose-Driven?

It is the hallmark of truly transformational leaders and teams to combine their ambitions and passions with their purpose. From a purely business perspective, it is proven that customers respond more positively to 'why' a company does something than to 'how' they do it.

Just like individuals, companies are living, breathing things that need a North Star and a sense of direction to thrive. Whys are aspirational and inspirational. They allow employees to clearly understand how their day-to-day work fulfils their company's purpose.

Take a moment and think about Apple's 'Humanizing Technology', Google's 'Organizing the World's Information', or Zappos 'Delivering Wow'. These aren't simply attractive words or catchphrases. But are, in fact, deeply rooted value systems that have turned these companies into the giants that they are today. The truth is, purpose remains at the heart of remarkable transformation. And there are tangible benefits to it.

Companies with a 'Why' Generate More Significant Profits

Research confirms that companies with a deeply entrenched why and clarity of purpose outperform the market by a whopping 9:1 ratio over a 10-year period. These purposeful brands and companies also radically outperform the stock market by 133 per cent, gain 46 per cent more share of wallet, and achieve results that are double those of average companies.

Have a Competitive Advantage

Companies with a deep-rooted sense of purpose develop the competitive advantage that comes with speedy execution. The why of an organization offers alignment and clarity and enables a company to stay agile, act fast, and work as an organic whole instead of disconcerted parts playing catch-up.

In other words, purpose eliminates red tape and ensures that everyone is laser-focused on the same objectives. This is why it's also easy to understand why employees in such companies bond better with one another and have great working relationships, making their work more meaningful and fulfilling.

Increase Stakeholder Loyalty

Companies that are internally and externally aligned and focused on their 'why' tend to have higher loyalty from their most crucial stakeholders: their employees and customers. Let's take the example of Harley-Davidson. Do they make the best bikes? Probably. But more than that, what matters is that the company is focused on fulfilling dreams of personal freedom, which drives internal and external alignment. The net result? Margins drive up, stakeholder retention rate increases, and the Harley-Davidson community thrives.

Attract and Retain the Best Talent

Purpose can play a key role in attracting top talent. Considering pay and other benefits are equal, people prefer to work with organizations with a vision and mission to change the world for the better. It is a great way to inspire exceptional work.

Create a Culture of Excellence

Creating a culture of excellence is the end goal and the net result of concerted efforts to rally your teams behind your company's why. In a setting like this, everything radiates from the inside out. When your company's culture is based on values and ambition, day-to-day work becomes a pleasurable experience.

But as you understand the value of rallying your team behind the company's why, it is important to understand 'how' to actually find your personal why. Your personal why, especially if you're a key leader within your organization, will help you and your team ascertain the why of your company.

Many people believe that a company's why needs to be similar to the products or services that an organization offers. It doesn't necessarily have to be that. A friend's company that is in the tech and IT industry offers vocational classes to women and makes a difference in the lives of many families in this way.

Another company that issues trading licences to businesses creates sources of potable water for people in various countries in Africa. Every organization can make a major difference in the world through their work.

> *Truly transformational teams combine their ambitions with their passion and with their purpose.*
>
> —John Doerr

In the early 2000s, Lucy d'Abo, along with her sister Camilla, co-founded DABO & CO, a boutique PR and communications agency in Dubai. What started as a small, ambitious venture quickly grew into one of the region's most respected independent agencies. Behind this growth was a secret weapon not often credited in business: an unwavering commitment to cultivating an exceptional workplace culture.

From the outset, Lucy believed that culture wasn't just an HR initiative—it was the foundation of a thriving business. At DABO & CO, culture meant clarity, consistency, and connection. The company fostered an open, collaborative environment where employees were encouraged to bring their whole selves to work. Leadership was transparent and accessible, and feedback was welcomed, not feared. This created psychological safety across teams and led to extraordinary creativity, client engagement, and retention.

As a result, DABO & CO attracted top talent across the region, many of whom stayed for years, growing within the organization. The agency's culture emphasized personal growth, work-life balance, and team celebration. Weekly team huddles, mentorship programmes, and regular recognition rituals created a sense of belonging and shared purpose. The company was named among the UAE's Top five in the Great Place to Work Index and won second place in Human Capital on the Dubai SME 100 list—a testament to how deeply culture was embedded in its operations.

This people-first approach didn't just make DABO & CO a pleasant place to work—it made it profitable and resilient. By 2013, the company had hit \$3.7 million in annual revenue, and its integrated communication model was being hailed across Asia-Pacific. In 2015, global communications giant Edelman acquired DABO & CO in large part due to its values-driven reputation and deep client loyalty. The merger formed Edelman DABO and marked one of the most high-profile PR acquisitions in the region.

But Lucy's commitment to culture didn't stop there. In 2021, she launched *Together* the Middle East's first consultancy focused entirely on workplace culture. Lucy now helps other organizations turn culture into their competitive advantage, just as she did with DABO & CO. She often says, "Culture is your superpower"—a belief that has proven true time and again in her leadership journey.

This case study exemplifies how a strong organizational culture can be a powerful strategic asset, fuelling sustainable growth, attracting top talent, enabling successful acquisitions, and even inspiring new ventures. It's a remarkable case that beautifully reinforces the core message of this chapter.

The Golden Circle and Its Significance vs Meher's Circle

The Golden Circle Theory by Simon Sinek explains how successful organizations think, act, and communicate when they start with why. Sinek is a leadership expert, and he shared this ground-breaking theory during a TED Talk. The Golden Circle allows organizations to dig deep and describe their value proposition to their target audiences in a way that differentiates them from other similar providers.

Leading and running a pioneering company is a huge amount of work. This is common knowledge. Unfortunately, what it usually implies is that most get caught up in day-to-day operations and the challenges that inevitably get thrown at us. It's easy to fight fires all day long until 5 pm, when it's time to wrap up.

We inevitably overlook what makes our company special. What is our company vision and objective, and why must we do everything we do in the first place? Many leaders are unsure how to respond to these questions. The Golden Circle provides a structure for addressing this problem.

The standard method for how companies process (and share) what they do is done in this order:

- What do we do?
- How do we do it?
- Why do we do it?

Sinek encourages everyone to flip this idea on its head and instead start with why and work back to what. Why is it more compelling? It evokes passion. Above all, what keeps you on your path even when the going gets tough? It's more than just a feel-good discussion about company values. It's an actionable framework that brings results.

The theory works because it is based on neuroscience. Humans respond best when messaging appeals to the limbic system of the brain, which is responsible for emotions, decision-making, and behaviours.

Go a Step Deeper and Discern 'Who' You Really Are

But what if we asked you to go even deeper than why and focus on 'who' for a moment, so you can emerge with your why as well as your company's? Because when you know yourself and who you truly are through self-love, you discern your most authentic self, which makes it easier to connect with your why or purpose. It then leads you to the purpose of your company and generally sparks confidence and teamwork within people across your company.

I believe that self-love and starting with 'who' remains at the centre of it all. It is very common for professionals across all industries to approach their work with a lot of aggressiveness. We keep telling ourselves to push harder, try again, and keep hitting until we win.

Compassion, the most important emotion needed for transformational and rapid success, is missing in interactions we have with ourselves as well as with the rest of the world. Any laxity in performance or results, and the biting critic in our heads begins its brutal commentary.

But those who succeed at a mental, emotional, and financial level cultivate a kind, uplifting voice within themselves that serves as a compassionate friend and guiding light. This is self-love and enables you to bring forth the best version of yourself. Moreover, the relationship that we have with ourselves determines the kind of relationships we have with others, including our most important stakeholders (employees and customers).

This is why your understanding of who you are will help you find your purpose. This will then lead you to discern the purpose of your company. And it is so much easier to spark the light in others when they see the fire burning in your soul.

Starting with 'WHO' will allow you to:

Become more courageous as a leader and positively impact your company's culture

This is a quality that enables leaders to take calculated risks and move outside their comfort zones. When you discern who you are with self-love, you essentially silence the constantly demoralizing inner critic. This way, you are more confident about taking a leap of faith and develop a stronger belief in your vision to succeed.

Enable your employees to be more authentic at work and bring their best selves forward

This approach also allows us to bring more authenticity to the workplace. We allow ourselves to be authentic and also enable our teams, employees, and people to operate from a place of deep authenticity. It allows them to do their best work more frequently and continuously work to push the bar higher in all areas. This sparks creativity, improves company culture, develops team spirit, and people find real joy in their work.

Make the journey extraordinary

Happiness, inner satisfaction, and true joy are not found in a future moment when all our goals are met. It can only be found now—in this moment. Self-love enables you to enjoy every single day. With this mindset, we tend to create happiness instead of waiting for it to arrive.

Start attracting and retaining top talent

As a leader, you already understand the importance of becoming a brand that attracts and retains top talent. Your employees are the driving force behind your company and play a key role in its success (or lack of it). By creating the right internal culture, you will consistently and regularly attract the right people who would be interested in joining and growing your business.

As they say, culture beats strategy every day of the week. So in essence, you end up creating a great culture by putting 'who' and therefore, self-love at the centre of your endeavours.

How to Establish WHO You Are

Most people lack clarity of purpose within themselves. A big reason for that is that you have lost touch with 'who' you really are at a soul level. As a leader at the helm of an organization, department, or team, you simply feel overworked but not always motivated. I can bet that your employees and colleagues also feel the same.

When people know who they are and are clear on their purpose, they jump out of bed in the morning and are excited to tackle the day. A continuous, beautiful feeling of joy stays with them. They feel passion, excitement, and eager happiness towards their work (and life in general). And because these people vibrate at a much higher frequency, they attract the right circumstances, situations, and other people. Here are the five key steps to determining 'who' you are:

1. Define your values

Your core values are the strong foundation that forms the basis of your personal philosophy. This philosophy governs all your life choices, actions, behaviours, and finally, results. Understanding your core values and beliefs will enable you to start to build the life you want. Just as every building needs a solid foundation, your core values serve as the foundation of your life.

To define your values, look back at your life and think about the times you took a stand, review the people and personalities you consider your heroes and delve deeper into the values they stand for. Soon enough, you will notice a common theme.

I defined my personal values about 10 years ago; they were love, honour, gratitude, forgiveness and service. These values were selected keeping in mind what was most important for me to feel, and also, at the same time, give to the world. Hence, they guide me in my choices, decisions, and many other aspects of life. I remind myself every day of these values.

Most often, we feel that we know our values and we operate with them in our mind; however, unless and until you have them written somewhere or express them to people, then it really doesn't work, and you won't be conscious about it.

Similarly, I was introduced to setting the company values after we, as a family, attended 'The Family Enterprise Challenge' executive education course at Insead with Randel Carlock.

Below are our company Palmon Group's values: love, empathy, respect, trust, integrity and success.

2. Reprogramme limited beliefs

A belief is simply a thought that you keep thinking. If you believe something to be true, then it will become your reality. Your brain cannot tell the difference between what's real and what's vividly imagined. So if you want to change your life, you need to first change your thoughts and beliefs.

The first step is to become aware of your limiting beliefs.

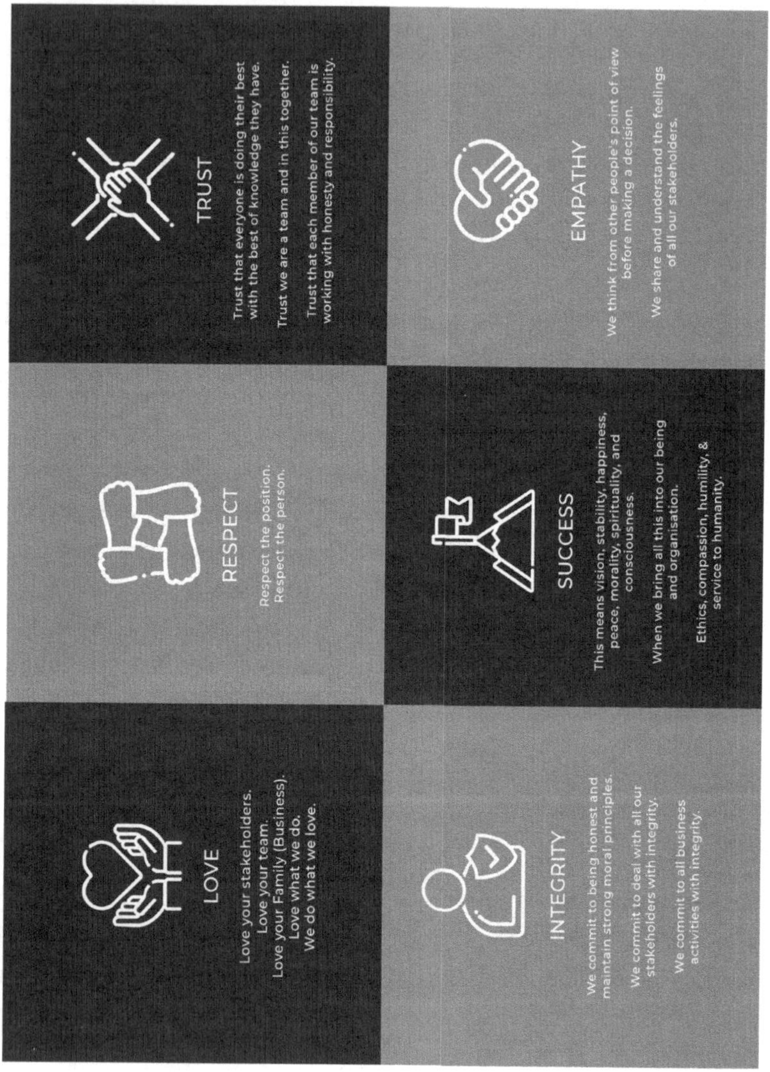
LOVE
Love your stakeholders.
Love your team.
Love your Family (Business).
Love what we do.
We do what we love.
RESPECT
Respect the position.
Respect the person.
TRUST
Trust that everyone is doing their best with the best of knowledge they have.
Trust we are a team and in this together.
Trust that each member of our team is working with honesty and responsibility.
INTEGRITY
We commit to being honest and maintain strong moral principles.
We commit to deal with all our stakeholders with integrity.
We commit to all business activities with integrity.
SUCCESS
This means vision, stability, happiness, peace, morality, spirituality, and consciousness.
When we bring all this into our being and organisation.
Ethics, compassion, humility, & service to humanity.
EMPATHY
We think from other people's point of view before making a decision.
We share and understand the feelings of all our stakeholders.

These are the self-defeating thoughts and ideas that are holding you back from achieving your goals. The easiest way to become aware of your limiting beliefs is to ask yourself:

What are my biggest fears?

What do I worry about the most?

What am I procrastinating on?

Why can't I achieve X goal?

For each of these questions, there will be a limiting belief attached to it. Once you identify your limiting beliefs, it's time to start challenging and reprogramming them. The best way to reprogramme limiting beliefs is through affirmations—also known as autosuggestions.

3. Spend time with yourself

In order to get to know yourself better, you need to spend time alone with your thoughts. This can be done through meditation, journaling, or simply taking some time out each day to sit in silence. When you spend time alone, you give yourself the opportunity to reflect on your life and figure out what you want to change.

It's only when we are away from the distractions of everyday life that we can truly connect with ourselves. Make it a regular habit done for a few minutes daily, and in the process, you will meet who you really are.

4. Live in the now

One of the best things you can do for yourself is to live in the present moment. This doesn't mean that you forget about your past or your future, but it does mean that you focus on the here and now. The past is gone, and the future has not yet arrived, so why not focus on the only thing that is real—the present moment?

When you live in the present moment, you are more aware of your thoughts and emotions. You are also more likely to make better decisions because you are not influenced by past experiences or future fears. The present moment is the only thing that is real, so make it a habit to focus on what is happening right now.

By doing this, you will also get closer in touch with your emotions and feelings from moment to moment and become conscious of the thoughts you want to listen to and those that hamper your progress and should be discarded.

5. Fall in love with yourself

One of the best things you can do for yourself is to fall in love with who you are. This doesn't mean that you become narcissistic or egoistic, but it does mean that you start to appreciate yourself for who you are. When you love yourself, you treat yourself with respect and care. You also become more forgiving of yourself, which leads to more inner peace.

Once again, journaling and meditation will come to your rescue during this process. Start by identifying the things you love and appreciate about yourself. Write them down and refer to them often. Also, make it a point to do something nice for yourself on a regular basis.

Your 'Who' Will Lead You to Your Purpose (Why)

As a leader, when you find who you are, it becomes easier to find your why and thus, create the why of your company. It has been proven repeatedly that authentic brands are built from the inside out and not the other way around. And those trying to simply communicate their way to greatness usually have a short shelf life.

The first great tip when you want to find your personal why is to immerse yourself in self-reflection. Think about what inspires

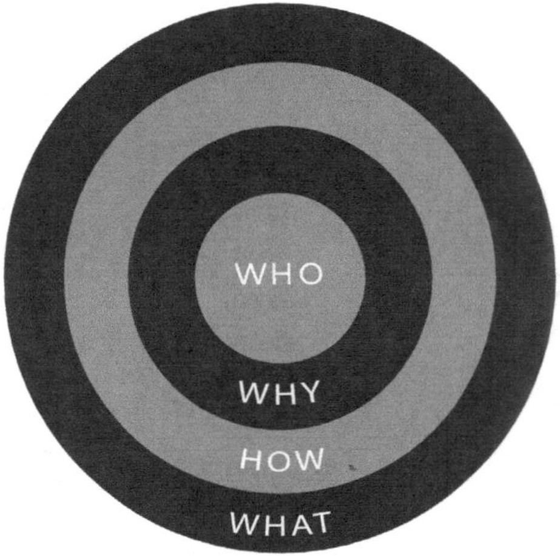

WHO

We are a family, we are together, we are love, respect and trust.

WHY

We serves future generations through education and support the Entrepreneurial Community.

HOW

We manage the premises so you can run your business.

WHAT

We own, acquire, and lease real estate, managing assets for SMEs and multinationals while operating a listed fund on Nasdaq to generate consistent returns for investors, balancing our commitment to both tenants and investors.

you to be at your best, or worst. Why is that? When reflecting on this, try to eliminate the facade we tend to create as we present ourselves to the outside world.

Next, take a look at your existing commitments. What do you feel about them? If you had a chance to shake things up, what would you keep and what would you let go of? Which of these will bring you closer to feeling more like 'you'? In other words, what would make you feel happier, freer, and on purpose?

It would also help to think in terms of the kind of change you'd like to bring to the world. Who would you like to help? What would you like to change? All of these questions will guide you to your why.

This is our company, Palmon Group.

WHO

We are a family, we are together, we are love, respect and trust.

WHY

We support the Entrepreneurial Community, we contribute to Educating Children, and we share to provide Shelter and Healthcare.

HOW

We manage the premises so you can run your business.

How we do it:

- Zero Downtime for your Business
- Experienced and Reliable Partner
- Enhanced and Upgraded Features

WHAT

We own and lease real estate, and we have a listed fund on Nasdaq to generate a consistent income for investors.

We acquire assets, we lease them to SME and multinationals, we manage them and service them.

Find What Sparks the Light in You

Start by making a list of all the things that spark a light in you. This should include everything that makes you feel very good about your life. Next, make another list of things that suck the energy out of you. Now, think in terms of how you can incorporate some element of it within your organization.

People are the most important element of the business for me. I love growing them and contributing to their journey to make them better versions of themselves, as I believe performance and success are by-products of who we become. I consistently invest my time and energy into growing the mindset of my workforce from blue collar to C-suite. I enjoy every moment of this.

Let Your Values Be Your Guide

Once again, it's time to look into the future and see the values you'd like to live by. These aren't necessarily the ones you are living by right now. Values are our compass and enable us to make the right decisions and do the right things in life. Personal values that move you deeply allow you to feel more connected to what's important to you. They make you feel alive.

This will also allow you to become clearer about the kind of values you want to express through your business. Eventually, this process will make your business more aligned with what drives you while simultaneously stamping it as being unique, even if you have many other competitors offering the same product/service.

Once I understood who I was, I was able to establish my personal purpose and reflect that within my organization. I became a coach, speaker, and author so I could impact fellow humans. This led me to create the Palmon Foundation through which we provide education and mentorship to young people in Bangladesh, Nepal, and India.

We support them financially as well as emotionally to be able to become better versions of themselves and contribute to their families and communities. I personally take care of this endeavour and have a monthly call with these young men and women where I talk to them about their challenges and guide them, so they stay in the right frame of mind as they work hard to transform their lives.

This enables them to stay in a mental state where they are victors rather than victims of their circumstances. Just last year, one of these youngsters graduated as an engineer. This year, one from the group is passing medical school.

People are only driven when they are serving. You are intrinsically motivated in life when you are driven by service, motivation, and contribution rather than fame and glory. This is because fulfilment will still be one step away if you focus on fame, glory and monetary success alone.

There are many stories where hyper-successful business owners and entrepreneurs longed for wealth and success, and when they finally reached their goal, they committed suicide. Success without the desire to contribute positively to society or other people has driven many people over the edge.

A recent case was that of HQ Trivia co-founder and CEO Collin Kroll, who overdosed on multiple types of drugs and committed suicide. The 34-year-old multi-millionaire was tired of the pace of tech and couldn't seem to keep up. When the hunger for more leads to an unfaltering focus on amassing money without adding the necessary value to your customers, stakeholders, or society, then it can create havoc.

Conclusion

We learnt that when we find our 'why' as a leader, it becomes much easier to ascertain the why of the company. I have highlighted two very simple ways to find your why and get a better understanding of how you can move away from what sucks the energy out of your life and move closer to the values that are in alignment with your dreams. But before you find your purpose, you also need to determine 'who' you are.

Once you determine your why and who, the next step is to inject that purpose into your company. When your company is purpose-driven, it becomes more profitable, and your people become more resilient. Purpose-driven companies are known to change the face of their industries.

Above all, you end up creating a culture of excellence that can, over time, make your company the best place to work, that attracts and retains top talent. Before you can do any of that, the first step is to go inside and find out 'who' you are.

Once you've become more aligned internally, it's time for us to use these learnings to align our stakeholders and customers.

ACTION STEPS

Reflection Prompt:

- Is my leadership rooted in purpose or driven by the need to prove, please, or perform?
- What parts of my journey shaped this?

Action Step 1:

Write one sentence that defines your *authentic WHY* (your reason for leading, beyond titles or targets).
Then write down one pattern or belief from your past that may be holding you back.

2: Does My Leadership Reflect My Inner State?

Reflection Prompt:

- When others experience my leadership, do they feel inspiration, trust, and love, or stress, urgency, and distance?
- How am I showing up energetically?

Action Step 2:

Ask a colleague to describe what it *feels* like to be led by you. Journal the insights.
Then reflect on how your inner self-talk is mirrored in your outer leadership.

3: How Can I Bring My Purpose Into My Daily Actions?

Reflection Prompt:

- What three regular tasks or decisions in my business feel disconnected from my deeper purpose?

- How can I approach them differently?

Action Step 3:
Choose one of those tasks and redesign it from a place of intention and alignment.
Note the change in your energy or outcome after trying this for one week.

Draw Your Golden Circle

Simon Sinek's **Golden Circle** begins with WHY and expands to HOW and WHAT. Let's add WHO to reflect your self-leadership lens.
On a blank page, draw four concentric circles:

1. **Inner Circle – WHY:**
   Why do I lead? (Your purpose beyond business)
2. **Second Circle – HOW:**
   How do I lead? (Your values, principles, and consistent actions)
3. **Third Circle – WHAT:**
   What do I lead or do? (Your business, offerings, projects)
4. **Outer Circle – WHO:**
   Who am I when I lead? (The version of you that shows up in the room)

Action Step:
Fill in your circles and reflect:

- Is my WHO aligned with my WHY?
- Where is the gap between my intention and my execution?

5

ALIGNMENT

Sharing Your Vision

Creating stakeholder alignment is not an obstacle to doing our job; it is our job.

—Doug Kessler

I'll never forget the day I sat in a room full of our company's senior leaders and felt like I was speaking a completely different language.

It was a hot afternoon in Dubai, and I had called a strategy alignment session after weeks of observing a clear disconnect between departments. People were working hard—there was no doubt about that—but they were moving in different directions. The marketing team was pushing one vision. Operations were executing something else. Finance was laser-focused on numbers, while HR was quietly drowning under employee disengagement.

As I began speaking about the direction I wanted us to head in—about creating a purpose-led business that would operate from love, values, and collaboration—I saw puzzled faces. Arms crossed. Raised eyebrows. One senior leader even asked, "Why do we need to talk about vision and values when we already have targets?"

That moment stung.

I went home that evening and sat in silence with a cup of ginger tea, reflecting on what had gone wrong. I had done the inner work. I had real clarity on where we needed to go as a company. But what I hadn't done was *communicate* it in a way that resonated with everyone. I assumed that just because I had clarity, others did too. But leadership doesn't work that way. Vision isn't top-down; it's built together.

That's when I was introduced to the Barrett Model of Organizational Consciousness. It changed the way I viewed alignment forever. I began to understand that to lead a 38-year-old family business forward, I first had to understand where we were on the map of consciousness. We were functioning in survival mode—just like I had been personally, years earlier, when I felt unseen, unsure, and just trying to keep things from falling apart.

The real work began with acknowledging that we needed alignment—not just in strategy, but in values, in purpose, and in how we communicated across the organization.

And I had to start with myself.

Just like with everything important in life, the only way to bring positive change in your organization starts with first understanding its current positives and shortcomings. Organizational Consciousness is a powerful framework that enabled me to evaluate the flaws within the Palmon Group. It gave me a high-level understanding of the issues within our family business. From there, we were able to slowly utilize different approaches to get better, more holistic results.

Every solution begins with a problem. But what if you don't know what the problem is? Richard Barrett offers a highly effective way to help organizations increase their self-awareness, understand where they currently stand, and then move up the ladder of success.

Self-awareness is one of the rarest of human commodities.

—Tony Robbins

Self-awareness becomes even more crucial when the future of an entire organization and its people depends on it. The Barrett Model, also known as the seven levels of consciousness, is inspired by Abraham Maslow's hierarchy of needs. It has been tested on thousands of organizations and is proven to be an extraordinary tool that determines the core values of an organization's leaders, employees, and partners.

All human structures, including your company, develop in consciousness in seven well-defined stages. Each of these stages focuses on specific needs that are inherent to the human condition. But with a full spectrum consciousness, organizations unlock unparalleled performances and are deeply cohesive with all stakeholders and derive a sense of fulfilment at all levels.

Full-spectrum organizations display all the positive attributes of the seven levels of organizational consciousness. The seven levels of organizational consciousness are powerful also because they symbolize growth by moving up. Without direction, there will never be any growth; hence, it is every important to understand why we need this evaluation and how to evaluate.

Level 1: Ensuring Stability
Need: Viability
Focus: Health, safety, profit, and financial security
This level is about meeting basic physical and organizational needs. It focuses on survival, ensuring the systems, structures, and people have the financial and physical stability required to operate.

Level 2: Building Relationships
Need: Relationships
Focus: Connection, respect, communication

At this level, relationships become central. It's about creating a safe, respectful environment where trust, open communication, and customer satisfaction are prioritized to foster cohesion and collaboration.

Level 3: Achieving Excellence
Need: Performance
Focus: Competence, results, quality
Here, the drive is toward high performance. Leaders and teams seek efficiency, accountability, and outcomes, building confidence through competence and striving to differentiate through excellence.

Level 4: Courageously Evolving
Need: Evolution
Focus: Transformation, empowerment, agility
This is the threshold of internal cohesion. It reflects the shift toward growth mindsets—welcoming innovation, personal responsibility, and continuous improvement in both individuals and organizations.

Level 5: Authentic Expression
Need: Alignment
Focus: Integrity, creativity, transparency
Authenticity defines this level. It encourages openness, trust, and honest self-expression. Alignment between values, behaviours, and purpose becomes critical for sustainable leadership and culture.

Level 6: Cultivating Communities
Need: Collaboration
Focus: Mentorship, community, employee fulfilment

Moving toward collective impact, this level fosters shared purpose and deep collaboration. It's about mentoring, coaching, and nurturing communities where people are seen, supported, and empowered.

Level 7: Living Purpose
Need: Contribution
Focus: Vision, service, long-term perspective
The highest level represents service to humanity and legacy. Leaders here operate from a place of vision, compassion, and contribution, driven by purpose rather than ego or profit.

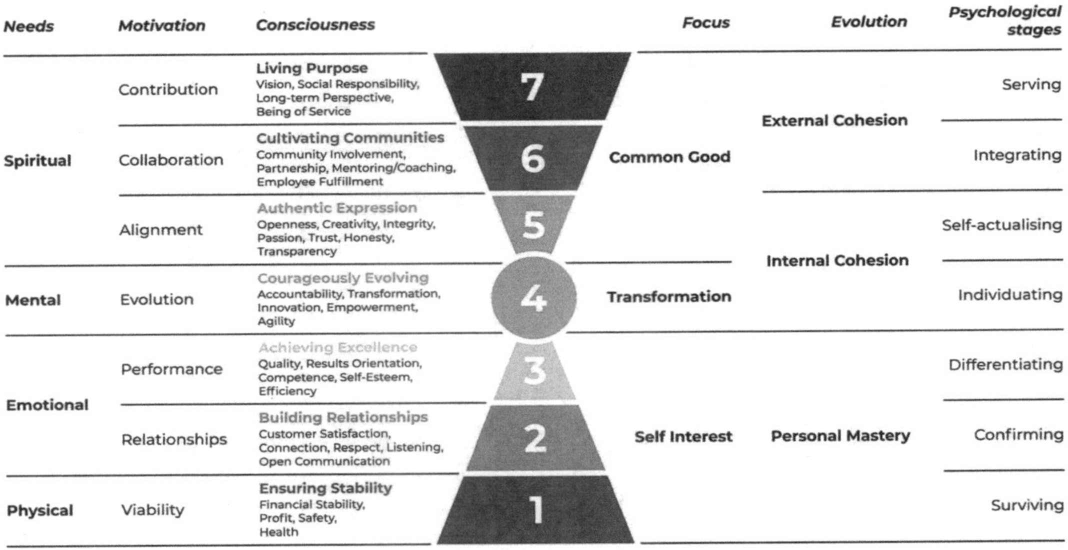

BARRETT VALUES CENTRE
CERTIFIED CONSULTANTS

SHERRINGTON
associates

Exercise To Be Done By the Individual or the Organization

When I joined my family business, we were at level one, and gradually, I have been able to move higher between levels three and four. While I understand from the model that when people or groups operate from the first three levels of consciousness, their sense of well-being will always be linked to the gratification of their deficiency needs.

Only when they have learnt how to satisfy and master these needs are their minds free to focus on the gratification of their transformation and growth needs, but steering my 38-year-old family business in the right direction is still a work in progress. My target is to move the organization and its people up to level five. I have introduced external coaching and mentoring programmes for team members to help them focus on internal growth.

At the end of the day, regardless of the type of organization you run, success depends on an employee's experience of the workplace and the leader's ability to inspire and motivate their teams, so that they unlock their full potential. Hence, I keep building myself to become a better version of myself to keep my family and team inspired to achieve the same.

Success is something you attract by the person you become.

—Jim Rohn

I've listed the four steps I started out with to understand where my company stood within the seven levels of organizational consciousness.

1. Determine where your company is currently:

The first step is to determine where your company falls on the seven levels of organizational consciousness. This can be done by conducting a self-assessment or hiring an external consultant to assess your company.

2. Set goals for where you want to be:

Once you know where your company stands, you can set goals for where you want to be. These goals should be specific, measurable, achievable, relevant, and time-bound.

3. Develop a plan to get there:

Once you have set your goals, you need to develop a plan to achieve them. This plan should include specific actions that need to be taken by your company and individuals within your company.

4. Implement the plan:

The final step is to implement the plan. This includes putting the actions into place and monitoring the results. Adjustments should be made to the plan as needed to ensure that your company achieves its goals.

Organizations that only focus on the lower needs rarely become market leaders. Although they may find some success financially, they are usually either too self-centred or too inflexible to be at the top of their game. In fact, almost 90 per cent of start-ups fail in their first year, while only 30 per cent of small businesses survive their first decade.

Their lack of ability to change with the times causes them to fall behind, and their employees do not feel adequately supported. They also often feel frustrated and stressed out. As a result, there is a general lack of motivation, increased turnover, and low morale in the workplace as a whole. These enterprises are frequently ruled by fear and aren't good places to work.

On the other hand, organizations that are solely focused on satisfying higher needs lack the fundamental business skills and capabilities necessary to function effectively. Their ineffectiveness and lack of practicality become apparent when it comes to financial matters. More often than not, these organizations are not customer-oriented and lack the procedures and methods required for success. In other words, they lack practicality and are far-fetched from the real world of business.

Therefore, the most successful organizations are those that operate from a full spectrum of consciousness. They create an environment of trust, have the ability to manage complexity, and can respond or rapidly adapt to all situations.

How a SWOT Analysis Helped Grow My Company

If you're running a company in a joint partnership or as a family business, a SWOT analysis will help you determine which partners should take up which responsibilities. In the case of my company, the Palmon Group, we conducted a SWOT analysis and found that my brother, Kunal Lahori, has strengths in his ability to execute tasks with perfection.

He was a natural fit to lead operations and legal. My father, Manohar Lahori, had a natural knack and finesse for finance. So, he took charge of the finance and banking aspect of the business. I'm very attuned to my emotions and those of others around me, and therefore, I was charged with the responsibility of hiring, people management, training, and growth. I also assumed the role of being a champion, so the responsibility of aligning the organization fell on my shoulders.

I knew what success looked like when we separated our roles in the business and understood that we had to trust and respect each other and follow the structure we had created. The material and other success we received as a result of this approach confirmed that when, as a leader, you know who you are, it's easier to get out of your own way and simply work towards the benefit of the company.

We figured out our strengths and weaknesses by putting ourselves through a process that included several meetings, countless discussions, and poring over tonnes of case studies. This helped us ascertain our strengths and establish our roles based on what we were passionate about and also good at.

Once we identified our core skill set as a leader, we then continued to invest in our education and learning. To this day, I regularly attend events and spend time knowledge-sharing with my mentors to deepen my knowledge about people management. As a leader, you have to keep growing in order to grow your people in the right way.

When meeting other leaders and business owners, I'm frequently asked how one can align individuals when every person is different. You can align everyone, regardless of how different their personalities may be, by showing them the company's values and vision, their unique role in achieving it, and finally, by being confident about the journey you are on. After understanding where you stand within the organizational chart, it's time to set up your North Star.

Your North Star

We have all looked to the night sky at some point and seen that one star that's always there, shining the brightest. It's called Polaris, and for centuries, it has played an astronomical role in guiding seafarers. It moves relatively within a small proximity just overhead the north celestial pole. To the naked eye, it is quite visible and appears stationary, making it easier for seafarers to find true north. All they have to do is look up at the North Star for guidance.

The same concept is applied in business when we set the North Star metric that Sean Ellis—a famous start-up investor—came up with. It is meant to be that one measurement most prognostic of whether a company is achieving long-lasting success. For a metric to be known as the North Star, it needs to do three key things:

1. Be able to generate revenue
2. Offering value to customers
3. Allow progress to be measured

When the metric is hitting all of these points, then your business will expand sustainably.

The Importance of the North Star Metric

The true purpose of the North Star metric is to get all the people working within the company on the same page. They need to know what the goal is to focus on achieving that and not get caught up in the irrelevant details.

But why the use of the North Star metric? Well, we all know that over 90 per cent of the existing global data was created within the past couple of years, meaning that an abundance of possibilities from an analytical viewpoint allows all the teams, departments, and contributors within your organization to come up with their own metrics.

This can lead to each team defining their goals differently, working against other teams, and as a result, duplicating their effort. To truly evolve your business and get out of a rut that will lead to collapse, it is important to set an intention, which is what the North Star metric sets out to do. It allows you to reduce administration efforts, simplify meetings, and ultimately, align the teams working within your organization with the same goal.

Also, it is possible to have more than one North Star if your business model is a bit more complex. Moreover, a North Star metric has several sub-metrics as well. In essence, it's just meant to simplify your company's strategy, putting it in terms everyone can understand, apply and remember.

How This Benefits You in the Evolution of Your Business

The North Star metric is essentially a guide for you. It's meant to be the compass that's showing you the path you have chosen to take and helps you stay focused on your main goals, such as success and growth.

There are three primary benefits of setting a North Star metric:

1. Though each team will have separate sub-metrics and goals they need to focus on, the North Star metric allows the company to work in alignment to achieve the same main goal.
2. The North Star metric helps measure organizational progress, meaning it will give a clear overall picture to everyone about how the company is doing. So, employees who might have been worried about the future of the company can be assuaged, meaning they will be able to reduce employee turnover and improve retention.
3. The North Star metric set will be the best reflection of the value you are bringing to your customers, which will help put you on the path to improve all the time. This, of course, will benefit you when it comes to customer retention and bottom-line revenue.

In essence, fostering this sense of alignment, transparency, and customer focus throughout the company through the North Star you set will help you grow tremendously and be a solid contender for the infinite game.

Finding the North Star Metric

The simplest way to determine your North Star metric is to decide what is genuinely essential for your business. Every company has its own set of unique challenges, and the reasons for its success and failure are manifold. Think in terms of which pillars of your business are the ones bearing all the load, and could lead to the company collapsing if they fail?

These are the pillars generating the most profit, measuring progress, and keeping clients happy. A metric that only focuses on making money without truly caring about satisfying customers will surely fail in the long term. The same is true if you only care about customers without making any profit, or setting one that isn't measuring how much you've progressed, because how else can you get insights to adapt behaviours and keep improving as you go along?

Here are some ways of ascertaining your North Star metric.

1. Ask yourself what is pivotal for the functioning of your business. Create a priority list.
2. Then, decide on the metrics and KPIs that can measure the key factors you've listed.
3. This will help you seek out the metric that encapsulates everything you've determined so far.
4. Then, build a hierarchy of your metrics, which is the North Star at the top of it all.

Much like seeds in the soil, North Star metrics require a fertile ground to reap results. Companies selecting their North Star will need the correct infrastructure and culture to see results. If cross-silo relationships are strong, and there isn't a willingness within teams to prioritize the good of the company over their own, then employees may end up rejecting the metric.

This is especially true if it requires a change in behaviour, or if, as is the case in most sales teams, the compensation structure acts as a conflict of interest. Thus, to align all your company members, it is important to have the right kind of people on board.

Conclusion

We have all, at some point, looked up at the night sky and found ourselves drawn to that one constant, unwavering light—Polaris, the North Star. For centuries, it has served as a guide for those navigating unknown waters, a symbol of hope and direction even in the darkest hours.

In business—just like in life—we need our own North Star.

Alignment isn't about getting everyone to think the same way. It's about helping people see the same vision. It's about creating a culture where every stakeholder, from the top floor to the shop floor, feels connected to something greater than themselves.

The truth is, you can't force alignment. You inspire it. And inspiration begins with clarity. First, within yourself. Then, with the people you lead.

When you, as a leader, embody the values and vision of your organization—not just in words, but in action—you create the gravitational pull that brings others into alignment. And when that alignment happens, it's magic. It's momentum. It's a team moving not in different directions, but in harmony toward a shared destination.

Never underestimate the power of one aligned, purpose-driven organization. It can outlast storms, outperform competitors, and outshine expectations.

Let your North Star be love. Let it be clear. Let it be the unwavering belief that your people are your greatest asset—and your vision, when shared and lived, can become unstoppable.

Because in the end, true success isn't just about what you build. It's about who you become—and who you lift along the way.

6
IMPLEMENTATION
How To Play the Game

Earn your leadership every day.

—Michael Jordan

A few years ago, during a particularly turbulent phase in our business, I found myself at one of the lowest points in my leadership journey. Cash flow was tightening, operations were stretched thin, and there were doubts in the air, both around and within me. The temptation to take shortcuts, make reactive decisions, or shift to a purely transactional mode of management was real. The finite game was calling.

But this was the moment my infinite game mindset was truly tested—and validated.

I remember sitting in a strategy review with my CFO and core leadership team, completely overwhelmed. I had built our company's foundation on vision, values, and culture—but in that moment, I wondered if they were enough. Would purpose-driven leadership stand tall in the face of mounting pressure?

That's when my CFO looked me in the eye and said, "Meher, you taught us that we're not here just to survive—we're here to lead with purpose, to build something enduring. Let's not give up on that now."

Those words grounded me. I wasn't alone. The values I had once only dreamed of weren't just slogans on a wall—they were alive in my team. It was in that room, with spreadsheets and worry lines, that I saw the power of alignment. We made some hard decisions, yes—but not from a place of fear. From a place of shared belief in the vision we had all committed to.

Together, we pulled through. And the real win? It wasn't just financial recovery. It was knowing that our culture had held strong. That we had built something far more powerful than a business—we had built belief.

In that moment, I understood on a visceral level what it means to play the infinite game. It's not about chasing quarterly wins. It's about nurturing a team and a system that can sustain and evolve through the highs and the lows. It's about building something that can outlast you, not just in structure, but in spirit.

Have you ever seen a successful company where the top leadership simply wasn't interested in becoming successful? Or a successful company where the employee churn rate was high, and despite that, the bosses were not willing to improve the culture? How about the successful company that had no vision or mission and simply wanted to make more sales, even at the cost of their customers' goodwill? You haven't seen these successful companies because they cease to exist, often just a few short years after birth.

Companies that grow huge and become super-successful aren't just those that innovate, but are also highly aligned at every level. Their partners and stakeholders understand the company's vision and mission, and stand behind them wholeheartedly. There's respect, trust, openness, and alignment throughout. And the culture is also great.

I will walk you through the importance of aligning with your partners and stakeholders (employees and customers), and why this can benefit your organization massively in the long term. I will also shed light on what an aligned organization looks like and how to get alignment within your company if it doesn't already exist. We will explore the seven levels of organizational consciousness to assess which level your company is at and the steps we can take to move the needle.

It All Starts with Ikigai

As a business leader at the helm of a family business or corporation, this process of alignment starts when you find your ikigai. It is a Japanese concept that means 'reason for being'. It's the thing that gets you out of bed in the morning and motivates you to do what you do.

For some people, ikigai is their family. For others, it's their passion or their work. For others still, it's service to under-served communities. Whatever it is, it's the thing that makes you feel alive and excited about life. Your ikigai or purpose allows you to define the company's culture. This is why ikigai is the first step. Once you've found it, you are ready to implement it within your company and unleash its full potential.

The Aligned Organization

How can you tell whether your organization is truly aligned? An aligned organization is one in which all members are working together towards the same goal. There is a clear sense of purpose, and everyone knows their role in achieving the overarching goal. There is a high level of trust and respect among members, and communication is open and honest.

If there's one thing that we have learnt throughout the history of modern business, it's that while ideas, inspiration, and inventions may come from individuals, long-term success only becomes possible through teamwork. And even if you put the most intelligent and the hardest-working people together, you can't expect anything great unless they are organisationally aligned and know the role they need to play in order to help reach it.

The best way to achieve this is to ensure that everyone has a clear understanding of the organization's purpose and how their role contributes to achieving that goal. Leaders need to set the direction and provide guidance on how to achieve the goal. They also need to create an environment in which people feel safe to openly share their ideas and take risks.

There are a few key factors that contribute to alignment:

- A clear and shared understanding of the organization's purpose through values.
- A commitment to working together to achieve the goal.
- A high level of trust and respect among members.
- Open and honest communication.

Why Is Maintaining Alignment Within Your Organization So Important?

You may say that plenty of companies around the world are going about their business without organizational alignment. That's true. But if your purpose is to grow your company and make it bigger and better than what it is now, then it's an area that shouldn't be ignored.

When alignment is missing, employees fail to recognize specific pain points. They may know they need to improve, but don't know what or where to start. A lack of alignment can cost your organization—sometimes heavily—in the form of a lack of agility, poor coordination, costly mistakes, negative influence on customers, lowering profits and sales, etc.

As a leader, keeping everyone on the same page isn't always easy. Your team members come from a variety of backgrounds and bring a multitude of good and bad experiences, emotions, as well as skills to the table. It is the hallmark of a true leader to have everyone moving in the same direction, rather than following their own agendas.

At the very basic level, it requires leaders to give attention to this aspect of the business and engage their teams through open and regular communication, lead by example, and practice inclusion. When your company is aligned at all levels, there are several benefits to it:

Improved communication and collaboration:
When everyone is working together towards the same goal, communication and collaboration improve.

Increased efficiency:
An aligned organization functions more efficiently because everyone knows their role and what is expected of them.

Greater innovation:
An environment of trust and respect fosters greater risk-taking and creativity, leading to more innovation.

Improved morale:
People feel good about working in an organization where they trust their colleagues and feel like they are making a difference.

Greater success:
An aligned organization is more likely to achieve its goals through intrinsic motivation.

Greater clarity around roles and responsibilities:
In an aligned organization, everyone knows their role and what is

expected of them. This clarity leads to improved communication and collaboration.

A sense of ownership and investment in the organization: When people feel invested in the organization, they are more likely to be committed to its success.

Building alignment within your organization is essential to its success. By taking the time to ensure that everyone is on the same page, you can create a strong foundation for your organization that will lead to greater communication, collaboration, innovation, and success.

The Steps to Get Alignment Within Your Organization

Real alignment happens when goals, strategy, and meaningful purpose come together. This gives companies a much clearer sense of priorities. This is how I implemented and maintained alignment in my organization.

1. Define the organization's common purpose and values: The first step is to make sure that your teams, customers, and investors fully understand the company's purpose. What is the organization trying to achieve? Why does it exist? Answering these questions will help to create a shared understanding of the organization's goals. From here, the next step is to create a strategy and brand identity.

2. Communicate the purpose: Once the purpose has been defined, it's important to communicate it to all members of the organization. Make sure that everyone understands what the organization is trying to achieve and how their role contributes to that goal. This process is most effective when done from the top down, meaning the top leadership needs to get fully involved. This is because company leaders better understand how each role within a company contributes to its purpose.

3. Set the direction and foster ownership: Leaders need to set the direction for the organization and provide guidance on how to achieve the goal. They should create a clear vision and share it with all members of their teams. It's important to remember that alignment isn't about positioning yourself a certain way on your website or the internet. It's about internalizing it as a living, breathing thing. If your leadership teams own their alignment, then it would become easier for employees, customers, and investors to align.

4. Create an environment of trust: It's important to create an environment in which people feel safe to openly share their ideas and take risks. This can be done by establishing trust and respect among members of the organization. In a few short years, millennials will make up 75 per cent of the workforce. And it's a generation that prefers collaborative workplaces and teamwork, and places a great value on companies that encourage a good culture.

5. Encourage open communication: Open and honest communication is essential for alignment. Make sure that all members of the organization feel comfortable sharing their ideas and concerns. Encourage feedback and have regular meetings to ensure that everyone is on the same page. For example, I am fully transparent with my team about my emotions and challenges, so I lead the way for them to open up.

6. Hold people accountable: It's important to hold people accountable for their actions and make sure that they are working towards the goal. This will help to keep everyone on track and focused on the organization's purpose. It also helps develop a sense of strong ownership within employees.

7. Celebrate successes: When the organization achieves its goals, it's important to celebrate the success. This will help to motivate people and keep them committed to the organization. It also makes them see that you value their contributions to the company. Acknowledge employees often, urge co-workers to do the same, and even bring different departments together by hosting social gatherings to celebrate teamwork and accomplishments. For example—we celebrate success every quarter, we award one member from each team for their performance and honouring the company values in all their communications.

Today's business environment is challenging, to say the least. A well-aligned organization is much better equipped to navigate the highs and lows of business and wield the power of alignment to differentiate itself from its competitors.

Playing the Infinite Game

Have you ever wondered why your business has seemingly stopped growing, and it seems much harder to scale than you thought? Real success comes from understanding the long game in business, as Simon Sinek aptly describes it in his book 'The Infinite Game'. Being a second-generation leader, it was extremely important for me to play the infinite game.

His concept is derived from a book by James Carse published back in 1986 and titled 'Finite and Infinite Games'. In this, the definition of finite games is those played by specific players, with fixed rules in place, and an objective that was agreed upon. The definition of an infinite game is one played by all kinds of players, with changeable rules, and most importantly, with the objective to keep the game going, rather than winning.

You have a stable system when a finite player is pitted against another finite player. Similarly, pitting an infinite player against another infinite one means the system will stay stable. The problem arises when a finite player goes up against an infinite one because the former is playing with the objective of winning, whereas the latter is playing just to keep the game going. Resultantly, the strategic choices that each player makes will be very different.

When playing against the infinite player, the finite player will always end up in a sticky situation. They would end up spending all their resources in the hopes of winning. Simply because of their short-term focus, they end up losing. Sinek gives the example of the Vietnam War, where the United States was fighting just to win, whereas the North Vietnamese were simply focused on staying alive.

This resulted in the US forces not exactly losing, but rather running out of the resources or the will to keep the war going and eventually dropping out of it. The same rule applies to the business landscape.

The minute you have senior executives obsessing about the short game, the game is lost.

—Simon Sinek

Within a business, you can have internal wins, as well as battles, but 'winning' business isn't a thing. Unfortunately, most business owners don't even understand the game that they are playing. They tell people that they're the best, they are ahead of their competition, and are at the top of their industries, but who decides that? What metrics and timeframes are these businesses looking at? It's all a self-created illusion.

When you play the infinite game with a finite player's mindset, there will be a gradual decline in innovation, cooperation, and trust. Eventually, the business won't have the resources or the will to keep playing the game, which is what we see happening all the time in the business world. The result is either bankruptcy, a merger, or an acquisition.

I relate to the infinite game because business, like life, is about enjoying the journey; that's the goal, and the outcome is a by-product of the process. If we focus on the outcome, we will miss the journey. I often affirm this in the family, whatever the end, now is what matters.

For us, the journey is one of learning, growing, being together and serving our investors with a consistent return on their investment in Manrre Logistics Fund. And we have the 'WHY', which is the Palmon Foundation, where we serve future generations through education. It's an ongoing scholarship that we provide to students in India, Nepal and Bangladesh.

It's about the legacy we live, not leave.

How to Play the Infinite Game

There are five main attributes, according to Sinek, of a player with an infinite mindset:

1. You need to have a 'just cause'. Really look at the why of your business's existence, and ensure you're willing to fight for something that matters.
2. You need to practice courageous leadership. It's the willingness to sacrifice short-term goals because you want to be here in

the long term. This is especially important if it entails caring for your people.

3. Creating a 'trusting team', one that fosters the kind of environment where people aren't afraid to ask for help or own up to their mistakes. When there is fear of punishment, it brings out the worst in people, and they lie, hide, or cheat. It's important to note that fear, stress, and burnout are all negative emotions and are the languages of the victim. You have to get out of this mentality to be able to take your employees out of it and take your organization to a victor mentality through alignment.
4. Setting a 'worthy rival' is important. It will reveal to you your own weaknesses so that you can learn from them and be a viable player in the infinite game.
5. You need to play by the flexible playbook, which Sinek refers to as the property of 'existential flexibility'. This refers to the capacity that you hold to cause extreme disruption to a strategic course or business model, if it means more effectively catering to your 'just cause'.

The reason I wanted to share these teachings from Simon Sinek's book is that they enable you to lead with love. When you lead with love, you will fight for a just cause, take courageous steps where needed, foster a trusting environment, look at the competition as 'worthy rivals', and practice mindfulness, which leads to increased flexibility.

Start-ups have their own challenges, young business owners have their own but a family business is unique in its challenges and very sensitive at the same time. A family business is not only about business, but also about family.

From my perspective, family is more important than business in a family business because it's your blood that you are up against, and monetary compensation can never buy you a family. Alignment, hence, plays an important role, aligning the intent, values and expectations of the family first, then the team members.

Conclusion

Leadership is not about "winning" business—it's about earning the right to play the game every single day.

When you choose to build a company that plays the infinite game, you're not just setting goals; you're defining a way of being. You're committing to a culture that outlives individual highs and lows. And most importantly, you're empowering your people to become co-owners of that journey.

When you're playing the infinite game, the journey becomes more important than the destination. It's about now. It's about having the best experience with your family members or team members now. It's about trusting now, having clear communication now, and celebrating now. It's about aligning now, so you can live your ikigai.

Alignment isn't a box you check; it's a living rhythm you cultivate. It shows up in the hard conversations, in the honest feedback, in the quiet courage of your team, and in the way your culture holds firm, especially when you're weak.

Remember, in the infinite game, there is no finish line. There's only evolution.

So lead with vision. Build with values. And play to keep becoming.

That's how you implement alignment.

That's how you earn your leadership.

That's how you thrive.

ACTION STEPS

What Is the Game You Are Playing?

What Is the Game You Want To Play? What Shifts Would You Want To Make?

7
THRIVE
Don't Just Survive

The best reason to start an organization is to make meaning; to create a product or service to make the world a better place.
—Guy Kawasaki, venture capitalist, CEO of Garage Technology Ventures

At one point, I remember sitting in my office, completely drained, and asking myself: *Is this all there is? Constant struggle, constant stress? Is this leadership?*

Then came a shift.

I realized I was surviving, not thriving. And so was the company. That day, I made a conscious choice to stop leading from fear and control and start leading from love and values. I stopped focusing only on outcomes and started focusing on the foundation—our culture.

The first change I made was to *communicate differently*. I opened up in front of the team and shared my doubts and struggles—not to seek sympathy, but to build trust. I told them, *"I don't have all the answers, but I know we can find them together."* That moment of vulnerability broke a wall I didn't know existed.

Then we co-created a new set of values—not in a workshop with fancy charts, but in raw conversations about what we stood for. We brought love into our dealings. Whether it was renegotiating with vendors during COVID, giving our staff flexible hours during Ramadan, or simply checking in with team members who looked low, we started showing up differently—human first, business second.

One of my proudest decisions was to appoint a "Culture Champion" in our team—someone whose only job was to ensure we were walking the talk when it came to values, empathy, and people-first practices. She became the bridge between departments and an early warning system for disengagement or burnout.

The turnaround didn't happen overnight. But it did happen. The same team that was once just going through the motions started to *own* their roles. Our operations stabilized. People smiled more. Solutions came quicker. There was energy in the building again.

We moved from surviving to thriving—not because of a new product, a new process, or a financial investor. But because we rebuilt the foundation with love, vulnerability, values, and belief.

I guess that you already know the importance of a building's foundation. It's the one thing on which the entire structure of a building depends. Without a solid, properly built foundation, the edifice can collapse. The same principle applies to your business. It is difficult to start a business, but the real challenge is ensuring that it prospers. This is why the foundation upon which you build your organization is crucial to its endurance and success.

If you've come so far in this book, you already have all the ingredients to make your business successful as a leader. All you need now is to focus on the correct values and practices that, when implemented, will give your organization a new life.

As you learn to set the North Star, lead with love, increase the levels of consciousness in your dealings and play the infinite game, you are slowly building an organization that is truly alive (and not just surviving).

Without these elements, you may still reach your financial destination, but it's unlikely to be a wholesome organization where every team member is energized to play their role and bring their whole selves to the table.

In this chapter, you will learn ten different ways to bring love and consciousness to your organization to make it a truly thriving and living entity.

Bring Life Back into Your Business

Here are some simple but highly effective ways to bring long-lasting and positive changes to your organization.

1. Communication within the Organization

The first characteristic of a great leader is that they communicate powerfully and effectively. However, it isn't enough to communicate. You need to focus on employing conscious communication and building a culture where members of your team embrace evaluation and debate that empowers them, makes them more receptive to feedback (given lovingly) and helps them feel safe sharing their ideas.

As a leader, you need to ensure that the way communication is taking place throughout the organization is in line with the company's core values. Whether your team is communicating with each other or across departments via phone, in person or email, the way they communicate needs to remain consistent with the shared values of the company. The best way to go about this is to have a guidebook or manual with communication-related best practices, which should be shared with all team members.

2. Being Vulnerable and Sharing the Pain

Most people believe that if a leader shares their vulnerabilities or discusses the challenges they face in the business or their struggles, they are displaying weakness. In reality, it is just a sign of humanness. When this kind of communication takes place, it creates deeper trust and better working relationships.

When you show vulnerability as a leader, it helps create a safe space for workers. It enables team members to feel confident that if they speak up, they won't be punished, rejected, or embarrassed, and instead respected and supported.

Project Aristotle

was a project launched by Google to understand the secret behind highly effective teams. They discovered that teams can work better when members feel psychologically safe. This was, in fact, the number one factor that was common in some of Google's top-performing teams.

3. Live Your Values

Living your values has cornerstone significance in leadership. Value-based leadership happens when leaders draw upon their values as well as those established for the organization for guidance, direction and motivation. An found that 94 per cent of its participants believed that a leader's values were essential for organizational growth.

However, it's not enough to just think about the values. As a leader, you also need to conduct yourself in a way that aligns with these values during meetings with stakeholders, on the phone and just about everywhere.

To do so, you need to drop your ego and judgement and be mindful of defensive or offensive attitudes or thinking patterns. This is the key to becoming a conscious leader. These values, essentially, allow you to play the infinite game. While the change starts with you as the leader, it should also be inculcated by your team. This relates to the point that was discussed earlier about developing a healthy organizational culture and aligning your entire business with your values.

4. Bring Love in All Your Dealings

Statistics confirm that since the pandemic, meetings have increased by over 70 per cent. This goes to show that we spend the majority of our time with the people we work with, and often the number of hours in this quadrant far exceeds those spent with friends and family.

To put it into perspective, we spend one-third of our lives at work. As leaders, we need to incorporate and develop a loving and patient way of dealing with challenges at work, especially when dealing with other people. It's the same way we deal with problems at home.

You need to be authentic, and to do that, you have to be the same person you are at home with those you work with. Understanding, compassion, communication and compromise are the main components of love, and all of these are needed to be an effective business leader. When you conduct yourself with love, you will create a safe space for all parties to reach their goals in a mutually beneficial way.

This reminds me of an incident that took place during the height of COVID-19. Just like many other businesses around the world, it was an uncertain time for the Palmon Group as well. One of our tenants wanted to terminate a long-term contract and was pressuring us to renegotiate the rentals. This went against our initial agreement and what was in the contract.

At the same time, I realized that if we were to nullify the contract and ask them to vacate, any other tenant would pay us a much lower rental. So, instead of pushing them out, why not offer a lower rental rate to our existing customers and hold them? And we did just that. This allowed them to complete their contract and enabled both parties to have a great relationship till the end. In this deal, just like I always do with all others, I put my ego and judgement aside and worked from a place of love. And everyone benefited.

5. Maintain a Deep Relationship with the Self and Others

Loving yourself is a critical human need, one that has enormous power to control your well-being. When self-love and acceptance are missing, we rely on other people to inject us with self-worth and confidence. In this situation, it is challenging to develop loving and healthy relationships with others because our internal states are out of balance.

As a leader, it is essential to develop a healthy, loving relationship with ourselves so we can thrive in our relationships with others. Leaders who seek to build personalized relationships with their teams and other employees also tend to develop deeper and stronger bonds through relatability and transparency.

6. Invest in Yourself as a Leader

"To value something goes beyond regarding or feeling that it's important. You also appreciate its qualities, while investing time, energy, effort, and sacrifice in its maintenance." This quote by Dr Steven Stosny resonated with me and goes to show what I already knew in my heart. It signifies the importance and value of loving yourself.

This rings true for exceptionally busy business leaders who often end up neglecting themselves or leaving their growth on the back burner due to pressure, lack of time, urgent business problems, etc.

This piece of advice is life-transforming. You can single-handedly change your business and your life if you invest time in continuous learning. Self-improvement is not something you can risk procrastinating on. This can include connecting regularly with mentors, reading, and opening yourself up to new ideas.

There are several reasons why this is necessary. Personal growth and development increase productivity, reduce stress, enhance resilience and happiness, improve self-awareness and control, help you build stronger professional relationships, make it easier to set clear goals and make you a better leader. When you become someone you aspire to be, you will inspire everyone around you.

7. Tap into Your Emotional Intelligence as a Leader

Tapping into your emotional intelligence and constantly working to expand it is important if you want to become an aspirational leader that your team readily follows and admires. Understand that your first responsibility is towards your team, partners, and then customers in this exact order.

As Simon Sinek says, customers can't love a company unless employees love it first. As a leader, your focus should be on creating more leaders. In our company, this is what we do. We strive for continuous learning and evolution, and that impacts and grows team members at an individual level.

8. Practice the Art of Detachment

We're biologically hardwired to avoid failure, no matter the cost. Due to this, many leaders struggle to control their ego when they fail at something. However, as a leader focused on evolving their business, it's important not to focus on the outcome. You can't be disheartened when results don't show despite your best efforts. When you detach yourself from the outcome, you can focus on doing the right thing.

This observation by Relational Psych director and experienced psychologist, Dr Carly Claney, helped me understand why it's crucial to healthily detach yourself while working. "Detachment is when you can recognize, acknowledge, and finally let go of emotions such as anger, hurt, or sadness, without becoming consumed by them. A healthy detachment creates space for a sense of objectivity that makes general productivity better, and in self-reflection, helps people explore their own needs. It's beneficial because by maintaining a sense of distance from events, one cannot be emotionally harmed by them."

To rise to the top, a true leader needs to rise above their emotions and ego, take failures as lessons, and use them for the betterment of the organization. This is also where love comes in. Instead of resorting to the blame game and finger-pointing, when you recognize that your people are on your side and everyone wants to play their role in helping the company flourish, you'll feel more empathy for yourself and your employees and use that to fuel your motivation instead.

9. Employ Loving Confrontation

Feedback is vital in business, but the way you offer it makes all the difference. Loving confrontation is key to keeping two-way communication alive. And at its base is the understanding that we are all human. Loving confrontation is also only possible when you genuinely believe that your team wants to improve.

Jay Hedley's *The Art of Professional Confrontation in the Workplace* shares a five-stage confrontation process that can make it a lot easier for you to handle confrontation lovingly. The first stage is preparation, the second is approach, the third is encounter, the fourth is back-tracking, and the fifth is conflict resolution. These steps can help you give and receive positive feedback and helpful criticism.

It's extremely important to help someone understand the crux of the issue, and not make them feel like an accused person. It's crucial to make others realize that it's not personal. And as a leader, you need to honestly care about the betterment of your employees for a loving confrontation to take place.

All of the points mentioned above will help you build your A-team for your joint performance and the future of the company. It will also help you have people on the team who are happy and loving and who love their lives. They won't burn out, even if they work hard, because they enjoy the process of doing business. When you prioritize your people (employees), it is tantamount to prioritizing your customers. And that's when your company starts to become truly alive.

10. Choose Your Champion

A final piece of learning as you transition your organization's culture and work towards improving it is to make sure that you assign a champion to lead with love. This person can be a C-suite executive, an HR person or an employee. Their role would serve as a bridge between various teams and departments/as they work to transform the company into a modern workplace. The chosen champion will educate and guide the rest of the company, helping to incorporate a great culture based on shared values. It is someone who will keep the company's focus on what's important and help inculcate the North Star.

I love how Gary Vee has a Chief Heart Officer whose job is to build the best human empire in the history of time. She is employed to manage talent, learning and development, communication, culture, employee experience and more. By this, they want others to unleash their greatness. How awesome is that? I have employed a similar person in my team, and we aim to provide similar services to our employees.

The Middle Ground Between Love and Leadership

I've had many leaders ask me this question: if you're leading with love and showing immense empathy and understanding, then how can you lay people off when they don't fit in within the culture you're trying to foster? Let me state the obvious first. Employees who fit in within the culture you're creating in your organization and successfully fulfil the roles they have been hired for will play a key role in your organization's long-term success.

Organizational culture is civilisation in the workplace.

—Alan Adler

Harvard Business Review published an extensive article on organizational culture and shared the role that working culture plays in nurturing and reinforcing specific thinking patterns and behaviours.

Therefore, if you have someone working for you who isn't aligned with the organizational culture, especially one that you're trying to build, it can put your company at risk. An out-of-sync employee can potentially negatively influence others, and as a consequence, their actions can affect your brand. So naturally, if you do end up hiring a person who isn't meshing well within the cultural fabric of your organization, you will have to let them go, believing that you are serving the company and the employee by doing so.

A huge lesson in love and self-love is the art of letting go of what is no longer serving you, or in this case, your company. This will also help you attract what (or more correctly, 'who') you're looking for. Thus, it only makes sense to show true love for yourself and those in line with the culture of love you've fostered and to let go of those who are not aligned with what you stand for and aren't serving your company in any way. It is also important to remember that cultures are promulgated from the top down. This means that the onus of creating a great culture rests on your shoulders as a leader.

WeWork: A Case Study

WeWork's case study offers a glimpse into what happens when your company's core values aren't set in the right way. WeWork started as a real estate company in the US and provided shared workspaces for tech start-ups. The company rose to prominence following the Great Recession and targeted millennials who needed co-working office spaces.

Adam Neumann and Miguel McKelvey became business partners. They rented an entire floor of a building in Brooklyn and divided it into cubicles, which were then rented out. As they gained popularity, they rapidly expanded out to San Francisco and Manhattan. They further scaled out into different cities after receiving an $8 billion investment from SoftBank.

Neumann was quite skilled at acquiring billions of dollars' worth of capital to grow rapidly. However, Neumann lacked a business model to assess its viability and sustainability, as well as proper expansion plans. They dipped their toes in other avenues, such as tech, and wanted to launch WeLive, which would be co-living spaces, as well as WeGrow, which would be a private educational establishment that his wife would run. None of these ventures sustained themselves in the long run. But still, WeWork was known to have the highest valuation within the tech start-up realm. Neumann claimed that he didn't care about making money, but rather, changing the world. Unfortunately, everything turned for the worse in 2019.

After over 10 years, WeWork filed for an IPO, which was meant to be a way to take it to new heights. Instead, they found an astounding downfall and capitulation. During that year, the company had to publicly file documents for the IPO, which was called an S-1. It exposed WeWork. The narrative of their unbelievable success and unimaginable profit was exposed, revealing the bizarre dealings, strange behaviours, and mismanagement by Neumann. They were immediately in hot water with the press.

The documents they filed revealed that they were losing a tonne of money. In the matter of just one month, WeWork's valuation dropped by 70 per cent. Since it failed, SoftBank ended up acquiring it, and Neumann was removed as CEO.

The question is, why did this happen? Firstly, their business model was unsustainable, and they were rapidly expanding. Additionally, Neumann's erratic behaviour and questionable dealings were cited as the two main reasons behind WeWork's failure.

With Neumann trying to create a creative working space that would attract millennials, the company was losing more money than there was coming in. There was no North Star guiding them. They were spending frivolously, without much of a profit margin. Neumann was known to be charismatic and great at charming investors. He would smoke marijuana, drink and walk barefoot around the office. But, there was more beneath the surface.

One of the many questionable personal dealings of Neumann was when he made hundreds of millions of dollars leasing several properties to WeWork, of which he was a part owner. WeWork was paying over $12 million for renting out spaces in buildings that Neumann partially owned. The former CEO was buying multimillion-dollar homes and taking 'personal loans' from the business so he could live lavishly.

Apart from the lack of a North Star, there was a questionable organizational culture reported. Neumann was using his private jet to transport marijuana across the border, and his wife was laying off people she got 'bad vibes' from. Neumann did not account for the needs of the company, and during times of need, would buy unnecessary things for himself.

Employees frequently felt burned out, and complaints were ignored. A former employee even filed a complaint for sexual assault and stated how it happened at several corporate events, and that HR didn't look into it. She was then fired based on 'poor performance'. A powerful quote from the victim further elaborates the importance of organizational culture. "The sexual harassment and assaults of the plaintiff did not happen in a vacuum. They are a product in part of the entitled, frat-boy culture that permeates WeWork from the top down."

Essentially, WeWork had become an extremely toxic place to work, with no proper HR department for months at a time. The company frequently offered employees the option to acquire stock instead of getting paid an appropriate wage. All of these reasons eventually led to the company's downfall. This showcases the importance of creating a solid and sustainable company culture, the value of keeping your employees at the forefront and playing the infinite game.

When we started the Manrre Fund, it was with a lot of enthusiasm and drive. We did the CSD listing on 3 March 2020, which was a very proud moment for us. But within 20 days, the entire world halted due to COVID-19. The uncertainty continued for two years. This was a time when we were all set to fundraise, but couldn't even call a single investor, keeping in mind the vulnerability they must be in.

We took this opportunity to build our culture based on our values. We welcomed new team members who shared our values, fostering a culture of love and openness. Additionally, we engaged external coaches to support individual growth among our team. It's not just about growing the company by solely meeting its financial targets. But it's also about developing the people because, as a leader, that's your job.

This process requires patience but will yield results you've never imagined.

Conclusion

Without these elements, you may still reach your financial destination. Still, it's unlikely to be a wholesome organization where every team member is energized to play their role and bring their whole selves to the table.

Love is at the core of all human beings. By inculcating love and bringing consciousness to all your endeavours, you enable your people to remain very loyal and faithful to your organization. A positive work environment and transparency go a long way when you are building and growing your company.

Always remember that money is a by-product of enjoying the process of doing business and growing the team members internally. It has lower energy, while love has one of the highest energies in the world. So, fostering loving energy within the workplace is important to attract and retain the right talent, build the best culture, serve people and eventually become financially successful.

ACTION STEPS

What do you need right now to Thrive? Reflect and answer the questions.

1. Leadership Foundation Check

- Are you leading from fear or love and values?
- How does your leadership impact your team's culture?
- Is your team surviving or thriving?

Action: Identify one fear-based interaction this week and change it to a values-driven conversation.

2. Live Your Values

- What are your top five leadership values?
- Do your team and culture reflect these values?
- How do you show vulnerability to build trust?

Action: Write your leadership values and share them with your team for feedback.

3. Appoint a Culture Champion

- Who embodies your company's culture best?
- How can you empower them to nurture your values?
- What support will they need?

Action: Choose and empower a Culture Champion to keep your culture alive.

CONCLUSION

Joy of the Journey

> "Don't ask what the world needs. Ask what makes you come alive, and go do it. Because what the world needs is people who have come alive."
>
> —Howard Thurman, theologian, civil rights leader, and mentor to Martin Luther King Jr.

Over the course of going through the challenges and obstacles of my professional and personal life, I've learnt a profound lesson. The only way to truly transform your life for the better is to connect with yourself, know yourself, appreciate yourself, and love yourself for who you are. Because only after that can you contribute to transforming and impacting the lives of others in a meaningful way.

This isn't just self-help advice—it's the foundation of authentic leadership. Compassion has the power to heal not only our wounds but also those of the people around us. As leaders, this is our greatest gift and our most significant responsibility.

And like they say, with great power comes great responsibility. To serve this responsibility, I embarked on the journey of writing this book. My mission is to serve fellow humans, helping them enjoy the journey, grow, learn, and contribute, so that we can build loving and inclusive relationships in the workplace. I want leaders to align their soul with their personality—to be the same person at home and work. I want us to carry the same energy of a loving parent, a compassionate sibling, and a caring friend into every boardroom and business decision we make.

This alignment of my personality with my soul, and my purpose with our company's WHY, became real in the journey of Manrre. After years of dedication, resilience, and vision—driven by deep hope and unwavering faith—we experienced a breakthrough in 2024. We partnered with GFH Partners from Bahrain, an institutional investor that not only saw but also believed in our purpose-driven approach. Their capital was more than a financial commitment—it was an affirmation that what we had built mattered. It was a symbol of what is possible when you build with clarity, integrity, and love. This partnership wasn't just a business deal; it was a moment of validation that when you lead with heart, the universe responds in kind.

Another profound example of this kind of legacy leadership is Al Shirawi Enterprises, founded by two friends—Mohan Valrani and Abdulla M. Al Shirawi—and now successfully stewarded by seven second-generation partners. I had the honour of interviewing Navin Al Shirawi on my podcast, and his clarity on culture, learning, and intuition deeply resonated with me. His words were a powerful reminder that super success is rarely ego-driven or rooted in fear. Instead, it stems from a conscious commitment to collective growth, guided by humility and deep trust in people. Their story is yet another living proof that when leaders think beyond themselves and align with values greater than personal ambition, they create institutions that not only endure—but inspire.

Yet, even moments of success are just milestones. They are not the destination. The real fulfilment doesn't lie in achievements or accolades—it lies in how you travel the journey. It lies in who you become along the way.

Fulfilment is not a trophy. It's a quiet joy, a deep knowing, a peaceful alignment of your inner and outer worlds. It's waking up with purpose and sleeping with contentment. It's being present with your team, with your family, and with yourself. It's the courage to live a life that reflects your values—even when it's inconvenient. It's in creating workplaces where people feel safe to be themselves, to be seen, and to be celebrated.

Our world today is not lacking in knowledge, talent, or opportunity. What we are lacking is connection. There is an impoverishment of spirit—a widespread hunger for belonging, authenticity, and compassion. And the truth is, we can't heal the world by scaling businesses alone. We heal the world by elevating the human beings within it.

Each of us plays a role in that. You don't have to be the CEO of a billion-dollar company to make a difference. You simply have to choose to lead your life from a place of truth and love. Whether you're a teacher, entrepreneur, parent, manager, or student, your alignment matters. Your healing matters. Your joy matters. Because every time one of us becomes better, the world becomes better too.

This book is an invitation to that possibility.

It's not a manual for perfection—it's a mirror for self-reflection. It's a guide that includes a practical workbook to help you reconnect with yourself, rediscover your company's purpose, and bridge the gap between your personal and professional lives. It walks you through the process of awareness, alignment, and action—so you can live and lead with intention.

Because here's the truth: we get sick alone, but we get well together. Fulfilment is a team sport. It thrives in communities, families, and companies that are built on love, trust, and emotional safety.

As leaders, we are not just driving profits—we are shaping cultures. We are influencing the quality of life for every person we lead. That's why love, connection, and authenticity are not luxuries; they are leadership imperatives. They are what will differentiate the organizations of the future—the ones that will not only thrive, but also endure.

So, I invite you now to make a choice. Not tomorrow. Not when it's convenient. But today.

Commit To Yourself.
Commit to knowing who you are and what you value.
Commit to healing what's broken inside you.
Commit to honouring your inner voice more than external noise.
Commit to being the leader your soul knows you can be.
Commit to building a life and a legacy that feels like you.

The world doesn't need more successful people. It requires more fulfilled people. More whole people. More courageous, conscious, and compassionate leaders who know how to love—and lead—with heart.

So go ahead—know yourself, lead with love, and leave a legacy that speaks not just of success, but of significance.

Because what truly counts is how many millions of hearts we touch while making the millions we aim for.

And that, my friend, is the true purpose of a leader.

ROAD MAP TO START YOUR JOURNEY TODAY!

This workbook is your roadmap—a space for self-discovery, reflection, and empowered action.

Take your time. Be honest. And remember:
Transformation doesn't happen all at once. It begins with a single conscious step.

Chapter 1: Awareness – Awakening to Self
Reflection:

- What is one moment in your life when you felt truly alive?
- What is your current definition of success?

Action:

- Write a letter to your younger self. What wisdom would you offer?

Chapter 2: Acceptance – The Mirror Within
Reflection:

- What beliefs about yourself have held you back the most?
- Where do you need to practice more self-compassion?

Action:

- Start a "Self-Love Journal" with three things you appreciate about yourself each day.

Chapter 3: Understanding – Rewriting the Story

Reflection:

- What story do you tell yourself about your past?
- How has that story shaped your present?

Action:

- Rewrite your narrative using empowering language. Read it out loud every morning.

Chapter 4: Purpose – Leading from Love

Reflection:

- Do your leadership decisions come from fear or love?
- What would change if love guided your leadership more often?

Action:

- Initiate one heartfelt conversation with a team member or loved one this week.

Chapter 5: Healing the Inner World

Reflection:

- What unhealed emotional wounds still influence your behaviour?
- Where can you forgive yourself or someone else?

Action:

- Write a forgiveness letter—whether you send it or not.

Chapter 6: The Power of Alignment

Reflection:

- Where are you living out of alignment with your values?
- What area of your life needs realignment?

Action:

- Create a values-alignment chart (Your Values vs. Your Actions) and address the gaps.

Chapter 7: Purpose in Action

Reflection:

- What is your WHY?
- What is your company's WHY? Are they aligned?

Action:

- Write a one-page purpose statement that connects your mission to your business mission.

Chapter 8: The Joy of the Journey

Reflection:

- What does fulfilment mean to you?
- Where do you find joy in your current season of life?

Action:

- List 10 things that bring you joy. Commit to doing at least three this week.

ACKNOWLEDGMENTS

This book would not have been possible without the quiet strength, support, and encouragement of those who stood beside me in ways big and small.

To my spiritual master, Shri Anandpur dham—your guidance has been the light on my path, reminding me to return to truth, presence, and love in all things.

To my mother, Reshma Lahori, my father, Manohar Lahori, and my brother, Kunal Lahori—your grace and resilience have been my foundation. Thank you for always holding space for my becoming.

To my husband, Anand, my twins Vaaniya and Vihana and my in-laws Moolchand and Bindu Khemchand—thank you for your unwavering support, your patience, and the love you extended so generously. You gave me the space to reflect, grow, and create with clarity.

To my entire team at Palmon Group, CFO Arpit Juneja, Portfolio Manager Victoria Younes, VP Admin and Govt Relations Raunak Lahori, Head of People and Purpose Ali Raza and Retail Director Poonam Chuahan… Thank you.

To the incredible guests on my podcast—your wisdom, vulnerability, and courage have deeply inspired this book. Each conversation was a spark, affirming the power of conscious leadership and soulful success.

To my friends, near and far—thank you for being my mirror, my grounding force, and my gentle cheerleaders. Your presence reminded me of who I am, especially on the days I doubted it.

To everyone who chooses to live and lead with intention—this book is also a tribute to you. May we continue to walk this journey of purpose, together.